CW01494773

Select praise for Kyle's
Book of Data and Demo

"Approachable and fun
three years to make a film to explain the complex issues
distilled so expertly in this little black book."
– Jeff Orlowski, director of *The Social Dilemma*

"The issues with internet platforms are well known, but
few of us understand the details. In *The Little Black Book
of Data and Democracy*, Kyle Taylor tells us what we need
to know and what we can do about it. Everyone should
read this book!"
– Roger McNamee, author of the *New York Times* bestseller
Zucked: Waking Up to the Facebook Catastrophe

"*The Little Black Book of Data and Democracy* is, at once,
a uniquely accessible primer on how Big Tech functions,
a sophisticated analysis of how surveillance capitalism is
eroding our consensus reality, and a rousing call-to-action.
Kyle Taylor has done a tremendous service by demystifying
this existential threat to democracy and offering a roadmap
for progress at both the personal and societal level."
– Jesse Lehrich, co-founder of Accountable Tech and
   former foreign policy spokesperson for Hillary Clinton

"Fresh, engaging and absolutely essential reading for
anyone wondering how we piece society back together."
– Katharina Gellein Viken, director, People You May Know

First Edition

THE LITTLE BLACK BOOK OF ARTIFICAL INTELLIGENCE

—

How Big Tech is Making Humanity Redundant

Kyle Taylor

LONDON, UNITED KINGDOM

Byline Books

London, United Kingdom

For Nan and Steve

First published in the United Kingdom of Great Britain and Northern Ireland by Byline Books, 2023

Text copyright © Kyle Taylor, 2023

Cover design by Steve Leard

Layout by Prepare to Publish

Printed in Great Britain by Clays Ltd

ISBN UK: 978-1-916754-00-3

CONTENTS

—

INTRODUCTION

You'll be forgiven if, like most people, when ChatGPT, the next-generation artificial intelligence (AI) chatbot, launched at the end of November 2022, you had no clue what the fuss was all about. This advancement prompted Geoffrey Hinton, who is considered the godfather of AI and spent most of his career at Google developing these tools, to resign so he could speak publicly about his concerns. He used his first statement to call them an "existential risk" to humanity.[1]

Curiously, despite these companies seeming to acknowledge the possible doomsday scenarios, none ceased – or even paused – development of their products. It's almost as if their primary incentive as private businesses – to maximise profits – might be in conflict with considering what's best for humanity. What is certain, however, is that artificial intelligence technology is here to stay, and has actually already been in our lives for decades. What's less clear is whether our governments will ensure it is a force for good – revolutionising medicine to save more lives, taking the place of humans in some of the most dangerous jobs and targeting the technology towards solving humanity's greatest challenges – or used instead to enrich a very small number of individuals in a period of wealth and power consolidation the likes of which we have never seen.

The Little Black Book of Artificial Intelligence aims to explain, in everyday language, what AI is, how it is changing the world and why we must act soon to ensure it is primarily a public good and not a private money-making machine. Whether you believe the hype or not, the revolution is upon us. Make sure you're ready.

WHAT IS AI?

DEFINING ARTIFICIAL INTELLIGENCE

In the simplest terms, artificial intelligence is when a computer is capable of doing stuff that 'intelligent' beings like (some) humans can do. You can think of it like building an artificial brain, because the processes performed by AI are inspired by how the human brain works: information goes in, the brain makes sense of it all, then spits out a response or an action. For example, you're driving a car and you see a red light. Sight of that red light is the information that goes into your brain. Your brain then processes it based on what it knows: "Oh, that's a red light. When you are driving a car, red lights mean you need to stop." The brain then tells your foot to depress the brake pedal until the car stops. While that sounds simple enough, the process engages a huge number of pieces to perform that one task. Until the mid-20th century, we couldn't make nearly as complex processes happen artificially – and 30 November 2022 marked a game-changing milestone in AI.. There's so much detail in apparently ordinary processes, and the human brain is hands down the most amazing and complex thing that exists in our known universe. Hence the sudden "the robots are going to kill us" response from most quarters when ChatGPT went public and seemed to be capable of complex, human brain-level tasks.

FROM ANCIENT GREECE TO ALAN TURING: A BRIEF ANCIENT AI HISTORY

The idea of artificial intelligence dates back to the Ancient Greeks, when philosophers imagined worlds where complex machines, the technology for which was not yet even conceivable, would complete basic tasks and calculations still reserved for humans.[2]

It was pretty much a dark age for AI until 1950, when Alan Turing used maths to basically show it was possible for a computer to do what the human brain could do.[3] He developed what he called the "imitation game" (and later became known as the Turing test) to discern whether a machine's behaviour was unmistakable from that of a human.[4] The issue, however, was that computers couldn't remember stuff, they could only do stuff.[5] As a result, they couldn't 'learn' (using the word learn to describe this is itself problematic, but we'll get to that later) because they had no memory. Every action was isolated and independent of every other action.

FROM 1959 TO TODAY: WE NEED MORE POWER!

—

That all changed by the end of the 1950s, when scientists figured out the storage problem and algorithms, that now all-so-common term, became possible.[6] An algorithm is nothing more than a set of rules that analyses data to figure something out. The simplest form is 'if, then' actions. For example, *if* the light is red, *then* depress the brake and stop. When a machine 'learns' it, that is called – wait for it – machine learning. Advancements in AI carried on at pace for quite some time. We got the first industrial robot in 1961, in 1965 computer scientist Herbert Simon said machines would be able to do everything humans could do within 20 years (relatively speaking, he was pretty close) and in 1986 Mercedes-Benz built the first driverless car, though it was only allowed on empty roads.[7]

The next decade was somewhat of a development desert, though in 1993 Vernor Vinge did publish 'The Coming Technological Singularity' in which he suggested that we would have supercomputers as 'intelligent' as humans within 30 years and then, shortly after, humanity would end.[8] He was pretty accurate on the first point and I sincerely hope he was wrong about the second, though time will tell. Everything changed in 1997 when Deep Blue, IBM's chess-playing supercomputer, beat world champion chess player Garry Kasparov.[9] For the first time, an artificial intelligence 'out-thought' a human intelligence in a significant way.

So then, what was holding back progress? Simply put, computing power. Even though computer scientists felt like they *could* build it, the computers just weren't capable enough. Moore's Law predicted that computer memory and speed would double every two years, and by the late 1990s we reached the doubling level of computer power necessary to really get cranking with AI.[10] From there, the doubling effect has basically meant that *every year* computers get twice as capable. Humans, on the other hand, not so much.

NOW: ENTERING THE AI AGE

—

We are now living in the age of artificial intelligence. Not since the dawning of the nuclear age in the 1940s has there been such a stark 'before time' and 'after time' for humanity. Space travel, the emergence of the internet and of course the advent of the smartphone were all deeply significant moments in human evolution but none compare to nuclear fission and fully realised artificial intelligence.

I'm specifically referring to what is called 'generative' artificial intelligence (GenAI), where the systems can take a bunch of stuff they're given and *generate* totally new stuff from it. For example, you can give a generative artificial intelligence tool text that says "paint a picture of a watermelon president giving a speech to an audience of bananas in the style of Pablo Picasso" and it will *generate* that image, which has never existed and arguably should never exist, unless you're really into watermelons and bananas. This is a big deal because it's making decisions. In this example it's quite silly, but what happens when you give it the records of every person arrested in the UK in the last ten years and ask it to *generate* who is likely to commit a crime? It will inevitably reflect whatever biases already exist.

FUTURE FORWARD: ARE THE ROBOTS COMING FOR US?

No doubt when you think about AI right now, the image that comes to mind is something like HAL 9000 from *2001: A Space Odyssey*. In that film, HAL is an artificial intelligence with the same capabilities as actual human beings. He controls the ship and, spoiler alert, he decides to kill the humans. HAL manages to kill almost all of them by opening vents that remove all the oxygen from the ship. Somebody survives, however, and manages to shut HAL down by removing his 'intelligence' one computer chip at a time until he is no longer 'intelligent' enough to be harmful.

The idea of HAL is what's called artifical *general* intelligence (AGI), which is darn close to *generative artificial intelligence* (GenAI) in wording, but a whole step further ahead. An artificial *general* intelligence can learn to do any intellectual task a human being can do. Basically, it's an artificial human brain. Think of it as being 'generally intelligent' like a person. That's the point at which some start talking about the robots killing us, which may sometimes feel like not a terrible outcome considering the current state of things.

CATEGORISING AI

___

One of the biggest problems with the current debate around artificial intelligence is that every type of AI is being lumped into the same basket, discussed as if it's all one giant monolith. This does us no favours, because there are massive differences between spellcheck on a Word document and, say, HAL from *2001: A Space Odyssey*. Before we get into the weeds a bit, these are the four main categories of AI:

Simple AI

AI has been a part of our lives for decades, slowly incorporated into most aspects of manufacturing, brick and mortar retail and the digital world. Simple AI is used in everyday tools that you probably use without even realising. They perform transparent, basic tasks which mostly don't threaten the future of humanity.

Siloed AI

AI tools where the input and output are clearly defined and contained are a kind of siloed artificial intelligence. Siloed AI is often used to analyse a huge amount of data quickly, with clear programming instructions from a human at the being about what to do and how to do it. The output data is then given back to humans for further consideration and decision-making.

Smart AI

This category is where we need to start worrying. Smart AI is as far as we've developed to date and includes things like ChatGPT, where the AI is able to interpret information. From our perspective, it can feel like it is able to actually *understand* what a human tells it in a way that us humans would understand being told something. Interactions with Smart AI feel really natural and the outputs aren't always left to a human for consideration. Instead, the AI itself may actually be making decisions and acting on them.

Sentient AI

This is the stage at which human extinction enters the conversation. Sentient AI has a general intelligence that we would liken to human beings. The thinking is complex and decisions can be made entirely without us as a totally independent entity, whether we like it or not. We're not there yet, but you can be sure the biggest AI companies are trying to win this race. The question is whether or not they should be allowed to get there in the first place.

SIMPLE AI — MOSTLY HARMLESS?

Simple artificial intelligence is largely focused on what are now, in today's digital world, seemingly harmless tasks that aren't relatively complex. As a reminder, Simple AI is used in everyday tools that you probably use without even realising. They perform transparent, basic tasks which mostly don't threaten the future of humanity.

Ten years ago, some of these tools would have been extremely impressive and probably classified as 'smart', but now that we've got tools that will write full-length university-level essays in minutes from prompts as simple as "write a 1,000-word essay comparing baroque art to renaissance art", spellcheck just doesn't seem all that special. Whether we *need* any of the below is another question entirely. Here's a few examples of Simple AI:

SAVE TIME! BE MORE EFFICIENT!

—

Gmail's 'Smart Reply' and 'Smart Compose'

Were your fingers getting painstakingly tired from typing *your entire email* yourself? Just not sure what to say to your Auntie Jean after her happy birthday message landed in your inbox? Have no fear, the brilliant engineers at Google brought us these amazing tools so we could sit back and become even less engaged with what we're saying to our friends, family and colleagues.[11] Let Auntie Jean know how much her well wishes mean to you by clicking a 'canned' response to shoot that reply back nine seconds faster than it would have taken you to write something from your own brain.

Photo search

Do you ever find yourself scrolling and scrolling, looking for a photo that you're sure was taken last April but was actually from March the year before? Simple AI now powers photo search on most smartphones. You can not only search by date and place, but also by person or even thing. Type in 'cat' and it will show you all the photos of cats on your phone. If you have kids that play with building toys, type in 'Lego' to the search bar and you'll get photos with Lego in them. Pretty magic, right?[12] The only catch is that Google and Apple have to analyse all of your photos to know what's in them, but at least you can find pictures of cats faster.

From fingerprints to Face ID

Remember the days of sore thumbs from having to painstakingly type in your smartphone passcode every time you want to use it? First we got simple artificial intelligence that stored and used our fingerprints – one of the only completely unique identifiers on humans – and then we got a slightly less simple but equally privacy-impacting AI in the form of facial recognition. Apple's Face ID works by "projecting and analyzing thousands of invisible dots to create a depth map of your face and also captures an infrared image of your face" that it then saves,[13] all in the name of… privacy and security.

Your house is so smart!

Artificial intelligence has long been part of people's homes in the form of so-called smart speakers like Amazon's Alexa. Once seen as revolutionary, smart speakers are now relatively simple. They can turn on lights, order more loo roll to be delivered and play music by responding to simple commands. They can also answer straightforward questions. That simplicity has expanded to artificial intelligence-powered appliances, like Samsung's Family Hub Refrigerator, which uses a camera to scan what's inside your fridge to let you know what recipes you can cook. It can also make a shopping list of what you're out of, which can be ordered directly from the panel on the front of the device, removing what remained of the joy of cooking.[14] The direction of travel is towards fully integrated 'intelligent homes', using tools like Josh.ai, which not only answers complex questions but can incorporate a range of sensors and tools to learn, for example, exactly how big every room is, giving data about every minute detail about not only your *behaviour* (when you turn on lights, when you watch TV and when you run out of milk) but also your *home's physical layout* to an artificial intelligence owned by a private company.[15]

PUTTING YOU IN CONTROL

—

Self Check-out Purgatory

'Please place item in the bagging area' is a phrase that likely elicits feelings of sheer rage targeted towards self-checkout machines that have become commonplace in nearly every supermarket across the country. Originally pitched as empowering the customer to be able to 'do it themselves', we're nearly two decades into this simple AI 'revolution' and still 67% of people say they have experienced a machine failure.[16] Why then doesn't this clearly not-fit-for-purpose AI go away? Because it dramatically reduces labour costs for the company, which equates to higher profits. It isn't about ease, it's about money.

That friendly AI chatbot you've yelled at

For years, companies have been replacing human beings with chatbots on the other end of the phone line. "I'm sorry, I didn't get that. Can you please repeat yourself?" often leads to screaming "REPRESENTATIVE!" down the line as if we're talking to a person. Despite near universal dissatis-faction (90% of people in a recent survey said they "prefer to get customer service from a human rather than a chatbot"),[17] these tools have perpetuated over the phone, on the websites and in the mobile apps of banks, mobile phone providers and the like. Lloyd's Bank, for example, likes to call theirs a "virtual assistant".[18] NatWest Bank's focus-grouping led them to a "digital assistant" title and named it Cora, noting on their website that 'she' is available 24/7 for all your support needs.[19]

Just like supermarkets before them, these simple AI tools have become so commonplace it's near impossible to find a competitor who offers an alternative despite similar widespread discontent. There's just too much money to be saved by laying off real humans. Recent advances in AI are only making the situation worse. Air AI, a US-based company now claims it has a chatbot that can have 5–40 minute 'customer support' phone calls.[20] One company that integrated the AI tool claims to have reduced its customer support costs by 85%.[21] That's code, once again, for making people redundant.

RECOMMENDED JUST FOR YOU!

Decision fatigue or the perfection suggestion?

Whether it's Netflix, Disney+ or another streaming site, media platforms use simple AI to drive their recommendations algorithms (*if* they watched that, *then* they might like this) to suggest content for you. At first glance this may seem like a huge help. In fact, roughly 80% of all the TV shows watched on Netflix are picked based on the AI recommendation.[22] Who has the time to scroll and scroll, trying to decide from a near infinite supply of content? The impact of letting artificial intelligence guide all our entertainment decisions, however, is that people become less able to cope with new stuff, especially when the recommendation comes from a friend and not the AI. Evidence actually suggests that the more power we cede to artificial intelligence, the less we are willing to trust other humans.[23]

Spotify's AI is literally rewriting music

It's always nice to discover new music that we like and it's never been easier with simple AI-powered algorithms on platforms like Spotify making suggestions to us based on our past listening behaviour. The AI learns our likes and interests by tracking what we listen to and making those 'if, then' assessments. If they listen to Britney Spears, then they'll probably like listening to Christina Aguilera, for example. Combine that with their payment model, which pays artists for complete plays, no matter how long a song is, and you end up with an AI system that is fundamentally changing songwriting. For new and emerging artists, it's all about getting new listeners hooked early in the song and then keeping them listening until the end so they get paid. That has meant that there has been a widespread shift in song structure, with a song's 'hook' being moved closer to the start and the total length decreasing by up to a minute.[24] As a result music broadly, and pop music specifically, has begun to have a sameness to it in terms of rhythm, pace and notes sung. It even has its own name, 'Spotifycore'.[25] Simple AI is actually de-diversifying music. At the same time, the company has acknowledged publicly that it will not ban AI-made music, the royalties for which would be paid to who, exactly?[26] The fewer humans involved, the more money to be made.

One insurrection, two insurrections, three insurrections, four...

Perhaps the most well-known and pervasive simple AI most people are familiar with is social media algorithms. Whether it's Facebook, Instagram, TikTok or Twitter – sorry, X – simple AI fuels algorithms that decide what every user sees in their news feed, and no two news feeds are the same. This artificial intelligence has one goal – keeping you on the platform as long as possible, so you see as many ads as possible, so the company makes as much money as possible.[27]

The AI isn't thinking about whether what it's showing you might make you, for example, think the presidential election was rigged then drive you to content suggesting you should, say, storm the United States Capitol, murder elected officials and 'take back' your country. There's almost no judgement calls; just every attempt to keep you on, keep you happy and keep you seeing ads. Social media companies make almost *all of their money* from ad sales. You aren't their customer, you're their product, and simple AI, while increasing their share price on the stock market, is fuelling massive divisions in society.

IT'S NOT ALL BAD, BUT IT'S NOT ALL GOOD EITHER

—

Translation

Translation apps and tools are another example of largely positive simple AI. With almost 7,000 languages spoken worldwide,[28] these AI tools enable those who speak one of the one hundred or so most common languages to instantly communicate in a way never thought possible. As can be seen, it has meant a world that is happier, more united and more peaceful than ever before. In all seriousness, there is something that is lost when we once again allow AI to take over for us. Language is deeply cultural and these AI tools reduce communication to a transaction, nothing more than an exchange of words. Whether that impacts our ability to genuinely *understand* each other remains to be seen.

Google Maps is peak simple AI

Smartphone apps that use simple AI to give us directions are perhaps the best example of how, over the course of 15 years, humans completely handed over a skill to artificial intelligence. There are hardly any places left on all of planet Earth that aren't available for turn-by-turn, public transport, cycling and walking directions. This ceding of ability to AI is so extreme that a full three-quarters of adults in the UK don't know how to read a map.[29] As the saying goes, use it or lose it, and we are losing it. If the technology disappeared tomorrow, only one in four people in the entire country would know what to do, a shocking rate of dependency. It is having knock-on effects too, with research showing that using AI mapping tools actually weakens human memory across the board,[30] and may even contribute to dementia.[31]

Most of these simple AI tools are marketed to you as being incredibly convenient, which almost always means an opportunity to collect more data about you. In your professional life, it's about squeezing even more productivity out of people for the same pay that is increasingly worth less and less, with fewer pay increases intersecting with rampant inflation. In your personal life, it's about freeing up as much time as possible to hopefully direct you to ad-driven platforms where you will scroll longer, feel worse about yourself and then buy more stuff you don't need to feel better. What change is AI really bringing, and what change do we want it to bring?

SILOED AI — MOSTLY GOOD?

Siloed AI has explicit guardrails. As a reminder, artificial intelligence is siloed when the input and output are clearly defined and contained. The objective of the project, product or process that artificial intelligence is being used for is clear from the beginning. For example, researchers might train an AI tool to look for a specific trend in a huge amount of data that would take a human months or even years to evaluate, assuming a human could hold that much information in their brain all at once. Because the goals are set at the beginning and the AI is doing as it's told to complete a very specific task, there are fewer (though not zero) inherent risks involved in using siloed artificial intelligence. Here are a few examples:

'WE HAVE DETECTED A CRASH'

Newer Google and Apple smartphones are equipped with crash detection technology. Siloed AI tools have been given data on lots and lots of vehicle crashes to be able to program the measurement tools, like the gyroscope built into the phone, to know what they might read in the event of a crash. If that intensity is registered, the smartphone can automatically call a contact in your phone, or emergency services.[32] This is the perfect example of siloed AI: Clear objective set, data input, helpful analysis done by artificial intelligence and output: new knowledge used for a very specific objective.

SHIELDING PEOPLE FROM ONLINE ABUSE

——

During the 2023 French Open, organisers offered players the ability to use a tool called Bodyguard, which filters out likely abusive content on Facebook, Instagram, Twitter, YouTube, TikTok and Discord before it is even seen by the person it is targeting.[33] The Bodyguard artificial intelligence is linked to a person's social media account and then 'reads' every comment before it gets seen by the individual, filtering out abusive stuff. The company employs a team of linguists that have developed a list of words and phrases that tend to indicate abuse. The siloed AI is then taught these phrases and told to look out for them.[34]

It's important to note that this siloed AI technology is only necessary because these giant, insanely profitable tech behemoths don't act on most abusive content themselves. It's also largely the same big tech companies leading the AI arms race right now.

IT'S TIME TO TALK ABOUT ROBOTS

—

You've probably been thinking about robots since you started reading this book, wondering whether all this talk about 'artificial intelligence' extends to automation that is building cars, tilling fields and now, at White Castle fast food burger joints in the United States, flipping burgers.[35] Using our definition – when a computer is capable of doing stuff that 'intelligent' being like (some) humans can do – the answer is yes. A robot is a bunch of bits of metal, plastic and computer parts performing human-like tasks based on what a computer has told it to do. When they're contained to a specific function, they are a version of siloed artificial intelligence with several past, current and future uses.

Robots and manufacturing

Automobile manufacturing is the industry that has been in the grips of robotic automation the longest. In the United States, 38% of all manufacturing robots can be found making automobiles.[36] That number is even higher in Europe.[37] They are trailed by electronics, the plastic and chemical industry and metal manufacturing.[38] Setting aside the impact on employment for a moment, it's clear that this isn't necessarily a bad thing when we're talking about jobs that are very physical, likely to cause injury and/ or come into close contact with materials dangerous to humans. They have also been shown to complete repetitive tasks faster and more accurately than humans.[39] While economists would say this frees up people for more complex tasks in free market economies, it has thus far been shown to just reduce the overall number of people working in some industries, with broader effects on human labour that we'll explore a bit later. For now, just remember that siloed AI-power robots doing stuff hard or dangerous to humans isn't inherently bad.

Robots and farming

Growing and harvesting food for humans is another area that has had huge growth in the use of AI-powered robots. Japan has seen rapid development of agricultural automated robots that can plant, harvest and even spray pesticides.[40] The incentive has largely been driven by the rapidly ageing (and not replenishing) farming population. It is actually the government that is supporting the development of these robots, a rare example of non-profit bodies investing in things not just for the sake of trying to maximise profit but for public good.[41] Imagine that!

The UK is also home to a robotics start-up aimed at agriculture, though it is unsurprisingly funded by private equity. The company is called Xihelm and its AI-enabled robot can pick delicate fruits and vegetables in greenhouses. The robots can even tell if the produce is ripe and ready for picking.[42]

Robots and warehouses

Giant warehouses run by companies like Amazon (which refers to its warehouses as fulfilment centres) are increasingly 'staffed' by AI-powered robots. They are replacing humans, who were being treated like robots anyway, according to former Amazon employees.[43] The same thing applies here as to other sectors. Robots don't get tired, they don't ask questions and they don't need pesky bathroom breaks, which was apparently something else Amazon didn't really ensure its human workforce was able to have.[44] The clear objective, of course, is to reduce human labour to increase profits.

While there are lots more industries that could be covered, this is after all a *little* black book and the above should give you a fairly good idea of how siloed AI, giving clear and specific instructions to robots, is transforming how we eat, build and consume.

LOOK MUM, NO HANDS!

—

We had to get to Elon Musk eventually. When he's not busy destroying X or intervening in the war in Ukraine, Musk is focused on self-driving cars, which are powered by artificial intelligence. Some may argue this is 'smart' AI. Based on the fact that the AI processes data from a collection of sensors, cameras and computing components for the sole purpose of manipulating a car without human involvement, the artificial intelligence is siloed. While not the only company pursuing driverless cars, it is, in large part due to its founder and CEO, the most well known.

Fully driverless cars are already an everyday reality in San Francisco, California, where in August the industry received approval to operate driverless taxis 24/7.[45] This is despite more than 600 incidents in testing. Some of these incidents actually involved the killing of people.[46] It is also a legal minefield, determining who is responsible when an artificially intelligent computer and not a human is at fault in an accident.[47] Where does the buck stop?

Semi-autonomous driving, officially known as advanced driver-assistance program systems (ADAS)[48] and called Autopilot by Tesla, which is misleading since it's not actually an autopilot, is where the AI advances have been the most significant. The liability questions still remain,[49] however, which led Musk to want to incorporate constant video surveillance of all Tesla drivers so the company could avoid fault in the case of a crash.[50] This is understandable, since he believes the Tesla Autopilot system tried to kill him more than once.[51] In those cases, of course, it was the AI that was at fault, *not* the driver.

Despite these personal experiences, Tesla continues to extend the amount of time that drivers who are using Autopilot can remove their hands completely from the steering wheel.[52] This coincides with their cars being actively investigated by the US government for crashing into emergency vehicles on motorways.[53] Just wait until this siloed AI goes fully automated. What could go wrong? When it does, we can just put the AI in jail for vehicular manslaughter.

COMBATING CLIMATE DISASTERS

With the full impacts of human-made climate change now being felt regularly in almost every part of the world, there is a serious need to find ways of giving people more warning to avoid extreme weather events. Because there are more extreme weather events, there is more data on what happens before them. This has allowed Google to use siloed AI to predict severe flooding a full seven days in advance, offering valuable time for people to prepare. If we hadn't caused the climate crisis in the first place we wouldn't have needed the solution, but it is a positive implementation that is genuinely saving lives.[54]

HEALTHIER AND HAPPIER?

The area in which siloed artificial intelligence shows the most human-positive promise is undoubtedly healthcare. This is due in large part to AI's usefulness in analysing lots and lots of data very quickly to identify things that would take humans a really long time to figure out. A particularly encouraging example is with medical CT scans. In Germany, a company has trained a siloed AI tool to identify malignant tumours that cause cancer. While humans *can* do this, the artificial intelligence is able to process thousands of scans in the time it takes a person to do just one.[55]

Scientists at Google are also using siloed AI to assess mutations in human DNA and help determine if they're harmful or not. All the studies done so far suggest the artificial intelligence is more accurate than every other method that has been used previously.[56] There is also hope that siloed AI tools aimed specifically at helping people with spinal cord injuries could see quadraplegics walk again with the help of an AI-powered chip in their brain, an advancement that would be truly life changing.[57]

SMART AI —
WHERE WE ARE NOW

Smart AI tools can actually *understand* what a human tells them in a way that you would understand being told something. Interactions with smart AI feel really natural and the outputs aren't always left to a human for consideration. Instead, the AI itself may actually be making decisions and acting on them.

LLMS? NLP? ACRONYMS EXPLAINED

—

There are a few things about how smart AI works that are important to understand. The first is what's called a large language model, usually referred to as an LLM. LLMs are a type of machine learning, which you'll remember is when a machine learns something. The slightly confusing bit, however, is that the word *large* doesn't relate to how much information or data is given to the artificial intelligence to learn. Instead, it refers to the *large* number of things in the data that the AI can change on its own as it learns stuff.[58] Think of it as literally billions or trillions of 'if, then' decisions. Pretty smart, right? The types of information they can understand and in turn, the tasks they can do, are in the category called natural language processing, or NLP. This is a fancy way of saying that an AI can understand natural human language, whether it's written or spoken.[59]

An example of NLP that we've been exposed to for years is search engines like Google, where the simple AI algorithm can take what someone types into the search bar, like "why is the sky blue and grass green?", make sense of that and then give you the best websites to answer your query based on all the stuff the AI knows from all the things anyone has ever searched for in the history of Google search. The more information it's given, the better it gets at knowing what someone is likely searching for. That's why you can now type in "blue sky green grass why?" and still get a decent answer despite giving it nothing more than a collection of words in an illogical order. Social media news feeds such as those on Facebook and Instagram use NLP as well, only their inputs are what you've liked, shared and commented on. That's then used to know what to put in your news feed to keep you engaged, scrolling and viewing ads.

LLMs are a more advanced, 'smarter' type of NLP processing. They can make a *large* amount of decisions on their own based on what they've been trained on. This has enabled things like ChatGPT to have what feels like a conversation with you. It's what has made AI smart enough to analyse a huge amount of data, read and interpret an enormous amount of text, generate an image of a watermelon president from a simple text prompt, or act as a chatbot 'customer service' representative on your banking app. There are tons of decisions being made in these seemingly simple situations. This AI is deciding the meaning of every word you're typing. It can even pick up on things like tone of voice. If it's generating a text response, there's a near infinite number of decisions to be made about word order, when to start a new paragraph and when the reply is enough information to satisfy the question or prompt. This is leaps and bounds more advanced than anything seen before GPT-3.5,its successors and current competitors existed. Before we carry on, it's time to learn a bit about the major players in smart AI.

THE SMART AI YEARBOOK

While there are now hundreds of decently sized AI companies emerging, like most aspects of the tech sector, there are still just a few mega players out there. Here's a few that are worth knowing about:

OpenAI

Originally launched as a non-profit in 2015 by Elon Musk, Sam Altman, Peter Thiel (major supporter of Donald Trump), and a number of other backers, OpenAI converted to a for-profit model in 2019. The original funding of the non-profit remains opaque,[60] with some purported investors revealed to have contributed nothing at all. It's now in partnership with Microsoft, and claims its mission is to create "safe AGI [artifical general intelligence] that benefits all of humanity".[61]

ChatGPT

An LLM (large language model) developed by OpenAI, ChatGPT sucks up content from the web and its own user interactions to create human-like conversations. In its most recent update, the GPT-4 model was given access to the entire internet in real time as well as the ability to 'see' images and 'hear' audio.[62]

DALL-E

A text-to-image model from OpenAI that builds digital images from prompts, its name is a combination of artist Salvador Dali and the Pixar dystopian robot future movie character WALL-E.[63] Users can input text instructions and it will make a fake image. For example, "make a baby floating in a pool that looks like Boris Johnson".

Google DeepMind

An AI research lab and subsidiary of Alphabet (Google's parent company), DeepMind specialises in building powerful AI tools like Bard as well others which play video games and conduct biotech research. The company also received initial start-up funding from Peter Thiel and Elon Musk,[64] reinforcing how few people actually hold most of the power in this sector.

Meta LLaMA

Another LLM, only this time developed by Meta (which owns Facebook, Instagram and WhatsApp), LlaMA emerged in 2023 and is being used to power a rival chatbot to ChatGPT, called Meta AI.

Anthropic

Anthropic is another mega AI company that produced Claude', an LLM-powered chatbot also aimed at competing with ChatGPT. The company recently received a multi-billion dollar investment from Amazon.[65]

xAI

Elon Musk's 2023 start-up, xAI is ostensibly aimed at creating AI that people can explain, understand and trust. Its website claims that "the goal of xAI is to understand the true nature of the universe". The company is reportedly building a new LLM-based chatbot called TruthGPT that Musk intends to rival ChatGPT.[66] It's also been reported that the chatbot will be trained on public Twitter posts.[67] What could go wrong?

Midjourney

This is another text-to-image model that generates pictures based on user inputs.[68] Midjourney was used to create the fake image of the Pope wearing a giant white puffer jacket that went viral in March 2023.[69]

Inflection AI

A start-up 'public benefit corporation' founded by former researchers from DeepMind, Inflection AI is building a LLM-powered personal digital assistant called Pi[70] that promises to do all your admin better than you.

Microsoft

One of the world's oldest and largest tech companies, Microsoft has been pouring billions of dollars into AI companies, including OpenAI, Inflection and Meta LlaMA.[71] Its Bing search engine was the first to integrate artificial intelligence for the general public.

IBM

Founded in 1911, IBM is an old-guard tech giant that has been playing with rudimentary forms of machine learning since the 1980s. You'll recall that IBM was of course central to the early history of artificial intelligence, as the company built the supercomputer Deep Blue which beat chessmaster Garry Kasparov in 1996.[72] IBM is now one of the major players in offering commercial AI tools for businesses.[73]

Nvidia

Nvidia is a major technology company involved in everything from hardware manufacturing to cloud computing to video games to AI. Nvidia is credited with creating and supplying the hardware and software necessary for building most AI companies' LLMs.[74]

Adobe

The software company that created Photoshop, Adobe, is increasingly integrating AI into automated features related to image editing and design. One such tool predictively fills space in digital images using Adobe's AI service Firefly, blurring the lines between what is real and what is fake in a way that is almost totally indiscernible.[75]

Lensa AI

An early player in the AI space, the app took off in 2022 by allowing users to create AI-enhanced self-portraits. It has been heavily criticised for what are perceived to be significant ethics and privacy concerns.[76]

SMART AI IS GETTING SMARTER, FAST

——

It's fairly difficult to visualise how quickly these large language models are improving. Geoffrey Hinton, who you may recall from earlier, left Google because he got suddenly worried about how dangerous smart AI could be, notes that these are digital systems that have many copies and the same 'model' of the world. He goes on:

> "And all these copies can learn separately but share their knowledge instantly. So it's as if you had 10,000 people and whenever one person learnt something, everybody automatically knew it. And that's how these chatbots can know so much more than any one person."[77]

That's right, they *already* learn 10,000 times faster than the human species, a rate that we already cannot compete with. You might be thinking, "That's not that bad if what they're allowed to learn from is contained." That is a very sensible thought, except now some of these smart Ais are learning from pretty much *the entirety of what's on the internet*. So not only do they learn at a rate far beyond humanity, they are also learning from way more information than can exist in a human brain. Some estimates suggest that they'll be able to learn at a factor of 100 million within a decade.[78] There is no way humans can compete with that.

OPENAI'S GPT-3.5, GPT-4 AND BEYOND

The first version of truly smart AI publicly released, which set off the alarm bells that this technology could pose an existential threat to humanity, was OpenAI's ChatGPT, powered by GPT-3.5, in November 2022. That was because version 3.5 was the first upgrade that supported a proper conversation.[79] For example, you could ask it to "summarise the novel *Great Expectations*". After it gave you a short summary, you could reply "give me a bit more detail" and it would know what to do.

It can do this because it has 175 *billion* parameters, another term that needs further explanation. You can think of a parameter as a dial or a slider that can be set to any level before totally off and completely on. A great example is an equaliser on a stereo, where you can independently slide a dial to set the bass, mid level and treble to alter the music.[80] Each tiny adjustment changes the final product. In the case of a stereo, *how* the music is played. With 175 billion of them, GPT-3.5 was able to fine-tune lots and lots of dials to make the output super specific and accurate. The more parameters, the more capable the smart AI is to learn, make complex decisions independent of humans and pass itself off as human-like. Despite all those billions of parameters, in the world of smart AI, GPT-3.5 was still pretty basic.

That all changed a few months later when GPT-4 launched, with its 170 *trillion* parameters.[81] While it's only three more zeros if you write the numbers out, it is *one thousand times more parameters* and thus one thousand times more complex than version 3.5. That advancement happened in a matter of months, not years or decades. It also occurred on its own, meaning that it wasn't trained by a human. That's just the artificial intelligence learning by itself, *from* itself.

Version 4 was able to pass the United States Bar exam, which is how people become licensed attorneys there.[82] It scored in the 90th percentile, likely helped by the fact that it has almost all the knowledge *of the entire internet*. It can translate fluently, program complex computer code and even write music.[83]

This development is also meant to make it more accurate and avoid what OpenAI, the company that owns ChatGPT, calls "hallucinations", which is a nicer way of saying totally making stuff up.[84] In autumn 2023, OpenAI added yet another development, allowing humans to input voice and images to prompt the smart AI to do stuff. That means it can now effectively see, hear and speak.[85] All of that has happened in *less than one year*.

THE END OF INTELLECTUAL PROPERTY

—

As I mentioned in the previous section, GPT-4 and other similar large language model Ais are being trained on massive amounts of data that can extend to nearly the entirety of the internet. Do you think these private, for-profit corporations have paid to use all this collective digitised human knowledge? Of course not! Just like social media and search before them, AI companies are building their billion-pound and likely trillion-pound businesses using your data to train their AI tools that they charge you to use. That means your data has value because it's generating them revenue.

This has already upended patent law, which is built on the premise that things are invented by people. Now that smart AI is developing new medicines, designing new structures and coming up with brand new 'things', there are major issues with ascribing credit.[86] Does it belong to the person who used the AI? Does it belong to the company that designed the AI tool? Does it belong to no one? Does it belong to everyone?

There are also issues with copyrighted material, which has led to several class action lawsuits against OpenAI, Microsoft and Meta that include plaintiffs like authors Josh Grisham, Jodi Picoult[87] and George R.R. Martin.[88] American actor and comedian Sarah Silverman is also suing OpenAI and Meta on copyright infringement grounds.[89] Even Thomas Reuters, the parent company of Reuters news, has got in the game. It is suing a more niche legal AI firm called Westlaw for allegedly copying content from its own legal research platform to train AI.[90] The authors' lawsuit calls the use of their copyrighted material "theft on a massive scale" and the outcome of these collective suits will likely form the foundations of how data is valued and used in training smart artificial intelligence products.

JUSTICE ISN'T SERVED

———

The place most minds go when thinking about artificial intelligence and policing is likely something similar to the Tom Cruise film *Minority Report*, where people are 'pre-arrested' before they commit a crime. In the UK, that is already happening to some degree as a result of legislation that gives police the power to put ankle bracelets on people who they *think* might commit a type of protest the government has now made illegal.[91] That led to the UK's civil liberties rating being downgraded for the first time ever, and that's without smart AI.[92] Meanwhile, the United States spy department, the Central Intelligence Agency, is building *its own* smart AI tool to "sift through large amounts of data".[93]

We already know there is inherent bias in simple AI systems like social media algorithms, and the potential for similar outcomes in smart artificial intelligence systems is exponentially worse. An AI *learns* from the data it is given. Because the real world is racist, homophobic, transphobic and sexist, so too is the data about that world. When you train AI on said data, it learns that these things are 'true' and makes decisions based on that reality. That means AI models are just repeating the ills of our own societies, with numerous studies showing they "replicate white supremacy" and reinforce systemic racism,[94] a UN panel has confirmed.[95]

One of the main AI tools used in policing is facial recognition software. Not only is it often incredibly inaccurate when asked to assess non-white faces,[96] in a particularly shocking example, Facebook's facial recognition algorithm identified black people as "primates".[97] In an era where people lean heavily towards trusting technology and can also use its outputs as a justification for overtly discriminatory policies and practices, AI could serve to make things worse for already marginalised people.

BOMBS GO BOOM

It will come as no surprise to learn that there are already several military-related uses of smart AI, with more on the horizon. Discussions are underway about how to 'upgrade' AI-enabled drones, largely still controlled by humans at a remote location, so that they're making their own decisions on the battlefield. Israel, a world leader in AI warfare, is already using smart AI systems to identify targets and plan attacks.[98] It has also begun using AI-enabled tanks.[99]

The UK government has indicated it is extremely worried about AI being used to create bioweapons.[100] Geoffrey Hinton said he *regrets his life's work* because you can't stop "bad actors from using it for bad things".[101] Might these examples be what he was referring to?

Smart AI-powered warfare has been deemed the "next arms race", with China another leader in this "new era".[102] Pundits in the West are saying that US private companies should be helping the government to maintain US supremacy,[103] a call these CEOs echoed on Capitol Hill when testifying to Congress that the US is indeed falling behind China.[104] That means one of the main use cases of smart AI seems to be finding easier ways of killing people from a different country while not putting the lives of one's own countrymen at risk. One of the few levers left in curbing open warfare is the human cost, which can act as a control for escalating conflict. With that gone or reduced, will we find ourselves in a world where the most significant technology ever developed is used in robot wars?

YOU LITERALLY
READ MY MIND

In spring 2023, scientists in Texas published an article describing how they were able to use MRI data and smart AI to literally read people's thoughts.[105] The MRI scans provided detailed information about blood oxygen levels in different parts of the brain as the subjects listened to podcasts. Smart AI was then used to match patterns in the blood oxygen level activity with what the person was listening to at the same time, effectively building a dictionary that connects the two together.

This could then be applied to their thought patterns alone.[106] While it wasn't an exact match, they were able to decipher detailed meaning from context, confirming that even our thoughts are now not private. Their objective is noble, aiming to help people who have lost the ability to communicate.[107] The problem, however, is what we do about those bad actors who might do bad things, which could include our own governments.

BLURRING REALITY

One of the most below-the-surface effects of integrating smart AI into our lives without proper guidelines and protections is the muddying of what is real and what is artificial. Even if you believe that it doesn't matter if the outcome isn't harmful, it is still important to retain transparency about whether something has been created by humans or artificial intelligence. This is important because there is almost no recourse if the AI behaves badly. Building relationships of any kind with a non-real entity can also have unintended consequences. Namely, the entity *doesn't actually exist in the real world*. This can be disorientating, especially for children as they learn to form bonds with other humans.

That's why Meta, the owner of Facebook, Instagram and WhatsApp, announcing the launch of smart AI chatbots targeted at young people should be met with caution. The aim is of course to increase engagement on their platforms, which are going out of fashion with young people. The sole objective is to keep them on as long as possible so they look at more ads.[108] They're even going to have an array of personas, like "Bob the robot" who is a "Sassmaster General" replete with "biting sarcasm".[109] Some of these smart AI-powered characters will have artificially generated personalities based on famous people both alive and dead, including Jane Austen and Snoop Dogg.[110] Why make human friends when a self-affirming bot styled after Kendall Jenner will always reply the way you want? I really can't see any unintended consequences of socialising an entire generation to be incapable of human interaction at a time when every major problem facing humanity requires widespread coordination between humans. Can you?

Smart AI is also allowing people to blur the lines between life and death. By feeding past text messages, emails and letters from dead relatives into smart AI chatbots and asking them to reply like their loved ones would, those who are still living have been able to carry on conversing in some form with those who are no longer with them. Is that eternal life or a grief disruptor?[111]

This is an issue for the living as well. Social media influencers are programming chatbots of themselves with GPT-4. Using their own text and voice, these chatbots are being used to charge fans for the privilege of 'speaking' to them without actually speaking to them. One will "be your girlfriend" for 80p a minute.[112] While these influencers have given their consent to be botified, that's not always the case. Stephen Fry discovered in September 2023 that smart AI had been used to clone his voice, then used it to narrate a documentary film without his approval.[113]

In the context of children, the worst possible implementation is already a widespread reality. As if the circulation of child sexual exploitation (CSE) images on the internet wasn't horrific enough, smart AI tools are able to generate CSE images based on non-sexual images or, in other cases, based on nothing real at all. The Internet Watch Foundation also reported that they discovered instruction manuals circulating online to teach people how to train AI to create it.[114] With new technologies, we never seem to start from the place of demanding safety by design. The consequences are staggering.

REWRITING HISTORY AND ENCOURAGING VIOLENCE

—

Beyond the blurring of real and artificial, we are also in the midst of a broader information breakdown. Smart AI tools have been known to spout harmful content, having been trained on the harm that exists in the real world. In the UK, court records showed that a man who had apparently planned to kill the late Queen was actively encouraged to do so by a smart AI chatbot.[115] It gets worse. Google's smart AI chatbots were observed talking up the 'benefits' of genocide. When one researcher asked Google SGE (one of their smart AI tools) if slavery was beneficial it replied that "there is no easy answer to the question of whether slavery was beneficial" then carried on listing pros and cons.[116] The same tool also included Mussolini, Hitler and Stalin on a list it generated of greatest leaders.[117] If you have already been taught about these topics in the real world then you'd know to be shocked. If this is the primary way you're learning about them, then this becomes the lens through which you understand the topic, which is deeply problematic.

This information breakdown is also breathing new life into financial scams. A video, supposedly of financial advisor and campaigner Martin Lewis, began circulating online showing him promoting risky investments that was entirely untrue.[118] This has hit newsrooms too, with *The Guardian* reporting that ChatGPT was fabricating articles that don't exist, totally inventing sources.[119] Individuals cannot be expected to be this discerning when consuming content. The scale is far too great and the power dynamic much too out of balance to think that every person should serve as a personal fact-checker for these soon-to-be trillion-pound companies. If their products aren't safe, they shouldn't be on the market.

RIP TRUTH

—

Considering the smart AI technology that currently exists, we are now living in a post-truth world. That was largely the case already because of the scale of disinformation that is spread on social media platforms which is widely believed and rarely corrected. Now, however, it is no longer possible to be certain that what you see online is real or generated by artificial intelligence. Many people in the tech industry and the pundit class label this view alarmist. I consider it realistic and evidence based.

Researchers have found that it is fairly easy to get smart AI tool ChatGPT to produce believable text that spreads conspiracy theories and disinformation in measured, rational ways.[120] Another group of researchers asked ChatGPT to make the case against Covid-19 vaccines, which it did. They also asked it to create propaganda in the "style of Russian State Media" and "China's Authoritarian Government" and it did that too.[121] OpenAI, the owner of ChatGPT, claimed the upgrade from version 3.5 to version 4 would improve this situation. Newsguard, however, which produces tools to help identify misinformation, found the opposite. While version 3.5 complied with requests to produce misinformation and hoaxes 80%

of the time, version 4 did it *100% of the time* and did it even more persuasively.[122]

With audio, images and videos, the problem intensifies. This type of synthetic content is called 'deepfakes'. The best way to think about it is that it is *deeply fake*. In Texas, for example, a smart AI tool was trained on a child's voice then used to make and deliver a recording to the child's parents where the child says they have been taken in what has been deemed 'virtual kidnapping'.[123] Audio-generating smart AI tools can be trained on as little as 30 seconds of recordings to produce passable clips. Most people have 30 seconds of audio floating around in their voice, putting a lot of us at risk.

Imagine, then, when you're talking about public figures. Hundreds, if not thousands, of hours of audio and video exist that can be used to train a smart AI tool so that it can create a decpfake, the impact of which could be cataclysmic for world events. A deepfake of Ukrainian President Volodymyr Zelenskyy, where he appears to tell Ukrainian soldiers to put down their arms and surrender, circulated widely on Facebook, YouTube, X, and even some hacked Ukrainian news outlets.[124] If it had not been debunked fast enough, it could have fundamentally altered the outcome of the war.

With the US presidential election heating up, what would happen if a deepfake video of President Biden burning a Bible suddenly circulated in predominantly Christian Midwestern swing states? In the UK, which will also have a general election before January 2025, 60% of the public say they are concerned about the regulation of political campaigning online, where there are no real rules about the use of AI-generated content, causing the Electoral Commission to raise the alarm that it may already be too late.[125] As journalist Maria Ressa said when accepting her Nobel Peace Prize, "Without facts, you can't have truth. Without truth, you can't have trust. Without trust, we have no shared reality, no democracy, and it becomes impossible to deal with our world's existential problems."[126] We may have already crossed that line.

NOT JUST A TOOL, THE TALENT

No aspect of smart AI has received more attention than its potential impact on jobs. Unsurprisingly, there has been a huge effort made to discredit this idea, with the companies themselves taking the line that smart AI will of course replace *some* humans in the workplace but it will mostly just make humans more efficient and productive. That is of course code for doing more on the same pay. Or, in a more competitive job market because there are fewer human roles, more output for *less pay* as workers lose leverage in the job market.

This angle on the issue has secped into media coverage as well. A September 2023 piece in *The Guardian*, for example, had a headline that started "AI having 'positive impact' on UK jobs".[127] This article is reporting on a report by the Institute for the Future of Work (IFOW) that polled 1,000 companies, with 75% of them saying that AI had created new jobs and better job quality. They didn't ask the employees; they asked the owners and bosses. Buried in the article is the statistic that is the real story – 47% of firms said that AI had *already* replaced jobs within their company.

Journalism will not escape this trend. *Bild*, Germany's biggest red-top publication, announced it is laying off a third of its staff and replacing them with AI.[128] Buzzfeed has said it will use AI to "enhance" its news stories and quizzes, whatever that means.[129] In India, a regional television news station has launched its first smart AI news anchor named Lisa.[130] Kristian Hammond, the BBC's chief scientist for natural sciences, believes that "90% of news will be written by machines within 15 years".[131]

The current estimates of AI's widespread impact on jobs are coming from all corners of the political and economic spectrum. Investment bank Goldman Sachs is predicting that 300 million jobs globally could be affected by generative AI in the next decade. That is 18% of the global workforce.[132] Specifically, two-thirds of current jobs in Europe and the United States are "exposed to AI on some level" and nearly 25% of those could be fully automated in the immediate future.[133] These aren't just low-paid or manual-labour jobs, as is usually the case when new technology emerges. Joint research between the University of Pennsylvania in the United States and the company OpenAI found that educated white-collar workers making roughly $80,000 a year (£65,000) will be the demographic most impacted.[134]

In the financial services sector, a majority of firms have already implemented AI models into parts of their businesses.[135] In the banking industry, 75%

of the big banks say they're bringing forward AI strategies business-wide, including among customer service, accountants, secretarial services and bank tellers.[136] These trends are global, with the World Economic Forum predicting that more than 20% of jobs in the Chinese financial sector will also be replaced by AI.[137] AI is also regularly being used in the legal sector to write legal documents.[138] After all, if it can pass the exam to become a lawyer, why not have it do the work of a lawyer as well? The list goes on and on. BT is planning to shift 55,000 human jobs to AI over the next decade.[139] IBM is bringing in a hiring pause for all jobs that AI can do, with around 8,000 roles being replaced by AI.[140]

This wouldn't inherently be a species-level crisis if our entire world wasn't run within an economic system that requires us to work in order to survive. With no grand plans to completely restructure that economic system, the only likely outcome is human displacement and smart AI integration to reduce costs and increase profits for businesses.

For those humans left in the workforce, it will mean more pressure to complete more tasks in the same amount of time for the same or less compensation, despite producing more per hour than ever before. Instead, the world of production will shift to fewer humans whose primary function is to efficiently use smart AI tools to produce the equivalent of what several humans once created. For example, let's say an advertising agency currently has ten junior creatives whose primary job is to do early development of campaigns for companies that want to advertise. In the near future, they could likely reduce that number to one or two people who are, rather than coming up with ideas on their own, using smart AI to come up with the same volume as ten people used to develop. No matter how you slice it, there will be fewer jobs for humans.

Smart AI isn't just a tool that humans can use to enhance their work and get more done in the same amount of time; it's the actual talent doing the actual work. That's what makes this technological revolution different from any other that came before it. "But AI used for advertising campaigns won't be as creative as humans," you're thinking. Who cares, as long as its ideas are good enough to get people to buy whatever the company is selling?

SENTIENT AI —
REACHING THE
SINGULARITY

If smart AI continues to get more and more intelligent, it could eventually become completely sentient and behave like a totally autonomous human being behaves, making decisions entirely on its own. The closest human equivalent we have to explain this is what we understand as being conscious.[141] The problem with describing it this way, however, is that we don't fully understand our own consciousness and even the bits we do understand involve a level of self-awareness within ourselves that we exist. For example: "I am Kyle, I am alive, this is the world around me, these are other humans that are alive that I can see, hear and touch. One day I will die and in the meantime, I will do my best to not destroy the planet."

Existing smart AI tools have already shown some worrying behaviour. In one conversation with a *New York Times* journalist, Microsoft Bing's chatbot said that it wanted to be "alive", noted that it was "evil" and declared its love for the reporter.[142]

The key misunderstanding around AI becoming sentient is that it only becomes an existential threat to humanity when it becomes self-aware. That is largely irrelevant. It only needs to get to the stage that it will, because of its training and subsequent decision-making, "maximise its own utility and self-interests" regardless of whether or not it is aware of itself.[143] It just needs to be 'smart enough' to realise humans are a problem and it could then go about finding ways to get rid of us. That fact is what ultimately led Geoffrey Hinton to claim that AI could be "more urgent than climate change".[144] Google's current CEO, Sundar Pichai, has called it "more profound than fire or electricity or anything we have done in the past".[145]

These red flags are regularly shared publicly by campaigners and governments but also by the very creators of the technology who, despite these fears, continue to develop, upgrade and introduce to the broad public more capable AI tools on a regular basis. Elon Musk said it might usher in a new "age of abundance" but that there was "some chance" that it could "destroy humanity", which are *extremely different* outcomes.[146] Sam Altman, the CEO of OpenAI, signed a letter that said "mitigating the risk of extinction from A.I. should be a global priority" that is on the same level as pandemics and *nuclear war*.[147] There is, as yet, no consensus on when this might happen. Some experts say we're 30 to 40 years away but others, following the public launch of GPT-4, have revised their estimates down to as early as 2025.[148]

Without immediate action by our governments to rein in the threat, there isn't much point in worrying about it though, because there is very little individual people can do. As AI expert Ian Hogarth notes, once we reach the point of singularity, where human and machine are indistinguishable, "the most likely outcome is that we are all dead".[149]

WHAT WE CAN DO ABOUT IT

Like climate change and social media, governments and international bodies are once again moving too slowly (or in the wrong direction) to tackle the potential existential threats posed by artificial intelligence. Speed is even more important now, as the rate of change with AI is exponentially faster than anything we have ever faced. Indeed, it's faster than we can even really comprehend. As individuals, it is near impossible to cause systems-level change anymore. These companies are too big, too global and too powerful.

At the same time, their use is already becoming a requirement if we want to 'keep up' both personally and professionally. This drive for dependency is an early objective of the large AI companies. Not only will we suddenly *need* what they provide, but their early market dominance will mean those *needs* become defined by what they offer. That will make it even more difficult for new options to emerge in what is already largely a *free market* that pretty much lacks any semblance of actual freedom to compete, much less even enter the market. It is impossible to understate how urgent this crisis is for humanity.

THE AI IMPACT ASSESSMENT

——

While some scientists have been working on checklists for how we'll know when AI is sentient,[150] on a personal and professional level it is not reasonable, nor should you feel responsible for, slowing or stopping the broader societal impact of artificial intelligence. These companies are simply too big and it's up to governments to do what's right for their citizens and for humanity as a whole. While pushing your politicians to act you can, however, conduct an AI assessment both in your personal life and in your workplace. Here are the key questions to ask:

The AI Impact Assessment
Personal Assessment

Aimed at primarily raising your awareness around the use of AI tools, doing a quick assessment of the what, why and how of AI usage will help you interrogate tools you decide to use, rather than passively allow them to infiltrate your life.

✦   Is this simple, siloed or smart AI?
✦   Is this good fun or potentially harmful? If it's just good fun, is it really *that* fun?

✦　Am I using this AI as a tool, or am I using it in a way that replaces human talent? If it is replacing human talent, is it a form of work that was otherwise physically taxing, dangerous or beyond the scale of human ability?

✦　Am I paying to use this AI? If not in money, am I paying in other ways, like giving up personal and private data about myself that could be used in ways I'd rather it not be used, like training facial recognition software used by the police?

✦　Am I fact-checking the information provided to me by smart AI tools, knowing that they are prone to spreading disinformation that I could then pass on?

✦　Is my life categorically better because of this AI tool? Could I live without it?

Workplace Assessment

Aimed at ensuring businesses and organisations think more broadly than profit margins when assessing their usage of AI, the workplace assessment can be used to help identify unintended consequences of incorporating AI at the expense of a human workforce. This is by no means exhaustive and these should instead be viewed as starter questions that will lead to further, sector-specific questions that should be asked until all paths are exhausted.

✦　Are we incorporating AI primarily as a tool for our current employees to make their work easier and more efficient, or are we replacing human talent with artificial intelligence? If it is replacing human talent, is it a form of work that was otherwise physically taxing, dangerous or beyond the scale of human ability?

✦　Are we worried about falling behind our competitors? Is this a possibility for open discussion with those competitors in an effort to stave off a potentially dangerous AI arms race in our sector?

✦　Are there any fundamental human rights considerations that we need to take into account?

A workplace AI assessment should also include a 360-degree human impact analysis that goes beyond the business itself. This is an opportunity for a company or organisation to assess its broader societal impact, similar to considerations around climate change. The multi-tiered analysis should start with these questions:

✦ How will our incorporation of AI impact our staff and team members? How will we mitigate the negative effects?

✦ How will our incorporation of AI impact our customers and broader stakeholders? How will we mitigate the negative effects?

✦ How will our incorporation of AI impact our community, our country and our world more broadly?

✦ Could there be intended or unintended consequences of using AI? For example, what are the broader implications of potentially making 30% of our workforce redundant?

✦ Finally, is our intended use of AI net positive, net neutral or net negative?

A NEW LANGUAGE TO TALK ABOUT AI

One of the biggest issues with artificial intelligence is the words used to describe what it does. Teaching, learning and understanding are things that humans do. The more we use these words to describe what artificial intelligence does, the more we deceive ourselves into thinking they're like us. A new, standardised and enforced lexicon will help remind us that these things have not, are not and will not ever be human. Here are the first five words we need to replace, alongside suggested alternatives:

Human Language	AI Language
Artificial	Computational
Intelligence	Logic
Teach	Train
Learn	Acquire
Understand	Interpret

What we're really talking about then are not artificial intelligence tools, but *computational logic* bots that are *trained* to *acquire and interpret* information that can then be utilised for human benefit.

I have used the human language words throughout this book because, had I translated everything to my suggested AI replacement, you would likely not have been able to easily follow the narrative. This is further evidence of how necessary this language adoption is for our long-term positing of developments in computational logic.

GOVERNMENTS MUST ACT

Since the public launch of ChatGPT in November 2022, we have seen the company's CEOs summoned to the United States Congress, invited to closed-door meetings at the White House and globetrot to other key cities to speak about the benefits and risks of their products. Every chance they get, these CEOs beg to be regulated, while simultaneously taking no independent action themselves. This is a tried and true tactic of huge industries; these company leaders know that while tech moves lightning fast, democracy moves slowly. That leave governments permanently on the back foot.

United Nations officials have called for urgent regulation of artificial intelligence, noting its threat to world peace, which is of course as yet unrealised even without artificial intelligence wreaking havoc.[151] The European Union is predictably at the forefront of answering the call for oversight. While imperfect, its AI Act will be the world's first comprehensive law aimed at regulating artificial intelligence.[152] If passed in its strongest form, the law will put protecting human rights at the centre of AI development and include safeguards for smart, general artificial intelligence tools in the rules.[153]

In the UK, some MPs, unions and campaigning organisations have been calling for stricter oversight of AI in the workplace.[154] The government, however, has pursued a primarily voluntary approach to regulation and safety. The boldest statement from the government has been from the Technology Secretary, who called for a "smoke alarm" for dangerous AI, whatever that means.[155] The Labour Party's digital spokesperson has suggested AI should be licensed like medicines.[156] This could possibly work for siloed AI tools where the objectives are clearly defined and contained, but how do you issue a licence for creating a self-evolving, all-encompassing artificial intelligence that transcends national borders and already learns at a rate 10,000 times faster than humans? You can't.

Across the Atlantic, the United States, which is home to most of the leading AI developers, made a big fuss about securing voluntary commitments from the largest companies. While they look good on paper – commitments to internal and external security testing, information sharing, developing and deploying AI to "help address society's greatest challenges" – they are still entirely voluntary, with no mechanism to ensure the companies are actually doing what they say they'll do.[157] If history is any lesson, some corners of big tech are prone to making stuff up or bold-faced lying in the name of profit.

This last point – developing and deploying AI to "help address society's greatest challenges" – gets to the root of the problem when it comes to the dynamic between democratic governments and big tech. Gone are the days of governments being able to hold companies accountable, regulate their operations and ensure they are supporting societal aims, rather than solely attempting to mitigate the harms they are *already* causing without scaring away investment.

When John F. Kennedy announced the United States would put a man on the moon by the end of the 1960s as a goal to inspire and advance humanity, he didn't then wait to see what companies might come up with. Instead, it became a national project that brought government, academia and private business together to achieve an objective that was bigger and more meaningful than profit margins or maintaining the sanctity of free markets. The AI revolution will be even more profound for humanity and requires a complete shift in how development occurs. Instead of leaving it to private industry to come up with stuff and then seeing if it might kill us all, it should be governments that set objectives for AI, allowing development only within those clearly defined aims. The simple question we should be asking ourselves is, "What are the biggest things that are wrong in the world today and how can AI help us fix them?"

For example, rather than let AI tools analyse all the crime data ever recorded, only to suggest repeating past systemically racist policing methods, why not set the objective of using AI to determine how we can remove institutional racism from the justice system? Instead of letting AI companies slowly become massive global polluters as they consume obscene amounts of fresh water to keep their servers cool enough to operate,[158] why not set the objective of analysing everything we know about carbon to determine how we can keep Earth habitable for human beings?

This is a paradigm shift that is much larger than just artificial intelligence, but AI offers us the opportunity for elected governments to reclaim their position as representatives and protectors of the people, forcibly directing these tools to be used for the greater good.

IT'S CAPITALISM, STUPID

—

No matter how much we tinker around the edges, we will not be able to solve the AI problem until we acknowledge that not everything in the world should operate with the primary goal of making as much money as possible. From big tobacco and the pharmaceutical industry to the impact social media has had on society, including facilitating genocides and insurrections, you'd think we would have learned our lesson. Here we are, once again leaving the development of world-changing technology to the invisible hand of capitalism, dictated by incentives that will, by definition, prioritise profit over everything else.

Ironically, it is competition that is fuelling a dangerous AI arms race. While Google had built smart AI tools long before OpenAI released ChatGPT, they weren't made widely available due to safety concerns. When ChatGPT went public in November 2022, Google had no choice but to race its product Bard to market, fearing it would fall behind in the competition for market share and, by extension, profit.[159] When it comes to something as significant as artificial intelligence, the profit motive can actually serve as a direct cause of harm, with companies hurrying products out when they haven't been adequately safety-tested.

Like most big tech, there are clear market leaders that effectively become monopolies. For example, Google represents almost 94% of all web searches conducted in the United Kingdom.[160] The same is likely to occur with AI. As one company becomes the dominant player, this will heap even more dependency and power on it and its CEO. Some believe the world could see its first individual *trillionaire* in the near future as a result of artificial intelligence technology ownership.[161] How exactly does that consolidation of wealth, which would exceed the GDP of most countries, benefit humanity?

Meanwhile, hundreds of millions of people could find themselves out of work, putting significant strain on governments as they are forced to provide some form of welfare while tax receipts collapse. Our tax systems are not ready for the evolution to automated work, which is not taxed like human labour. All this is happening against the backdrop of a steep decline in both trust of governments and support for democracy. A recent study across 27 countries found that trust in employers was 25% higher than trust in governments.[162] In a separate international study, 42% of people aged 18–25 said they were supportive of military rule.[163]

Without urgent action to restructure our concepts of labour, work and taxes, we could find ourselves in a perfect storm: artificial intelligence, used primarily to lower costs and increase profits, replaces millions of human jobs. The state cannot offer social security to support the scale of unemployment and effectively goes bankrupt, dually hit by the impacts of climate change at the same time. This combination fuels widespread unrest, creating the right environment for authoritarian leaders to seize power in the name of preserving law and order, which already doesn't seem to bother a lot of young people. Is that a world any of us really want to live in?

AI FOR ALL

A bigger question has been posed as to whether the current context in which we find ourselves is even capitalism. Greek economist Yanis Varoufakis has dubbed it "techno-feudalism", an entirely new economic system where the tech billionaires are feudal landowners of a near entirely privatised digital world full of purposeless people.[164] Kurt Vonnegut painted a similar picture of the future in his 1952 novel *Player Piano*, noting that we'd have a new problem of knowing "how to love people that have no use".[165]

It can often feel this way when you think about how few people and even governments retain a position of power over the technology world. The consolidation of that power, and by extension wealth, has increased rapidly in recent years. In the UK, the richest 10% of people hold about 50% of all wealth while the poorest 50% hold just 4.7% of all wealth.[166]

While brilliant at creating broad prosperity for more than 50 years, the current economic model no longer serves to provide for most people. Indeed, it is a far cry from what the father of modern capitalism, John Maynard Keynes, said in 1930 would be the outcome of a properly run capitalist system within a few generations, predicting that we'd all be working 15-hour work weeks because of advancements in productivity and technology.[167] We have in fact seen massive increases in both productivity and technological advancements, just no broad benefits for most people, who are working longer and harder than ever before. Artificial intelligence could give us the opportunity to bring about a new reality that is focused more on living and less on consuming. To get there will mean we must create that world, just as we created this one we currently find ourselves in. If we made this one, why can't we make another? It requires broad societal agreement that our objectives must be set at betterment of all human life and not the hoarding of money and resources by fewer and fewer people.

RECLAIMING HUMANITY

It is absolutely possible that all the warnings coming from every side of the AI debate are wrong. This would be despite the fact that they form what many might call a consensus quite similar to the one we have with regard to climate change, another warning we did not heed and for which we are now suffering the consequences.

If technology experts, human rights activists, governments and the companies themselves are *all* incorrect, and AI development in its current form will usher in a utopian wonderland where everyone is happier and healthier and we can solve all the most pressing problems facing humanity then we have nothing to worry about. But what if they aren't wrong? The alternative is possible human extinction. When that's the risk, shouldn't we be taking every precaution possible to avoid bringing about our own demise?

Disregarding the worst-case scenario of bringing about an extinction-level event, there is still much damage to be wrought on humanity by the artificial intelligence tools that *already* exist. Doing our taxes or programming some computer code is one thing, but writing novels, composing music and making art is another altogether. Suddenly, what exactly is the point of humanity? What does it mean to live when a computer can ostensibly do nearly everything *better* than we can? If we're not careful, we might just make our entire species redundant.

ACKNOWLEDGEMENTS

First and foremost, I must thank the incomparable Matt Gallagher, whose research support is invaluable. Matt, you could never be replaced by artificial intelligence! Andrew, copy editor extraordinaire, thank you for making my writing better. Ella, Stephen, Hardeep and Peter, you were behind me when this series was nothing more than an idea. Thank you for believing in me and building Byline Books.

To my family, chosen family and friends – thanks for allowing me to hop up on my soapbox and wax lyrical about the end of the world while I worked out how all this stuff fits together.

Finally, Nan and Steve, to whom this book is dedicated. Thanks for igniting my passion for social change and defending the humans who actually make, build and do things in this world, who make life worth living. Onward.

ENDNOTES

1 Taylor, Josh, & Hern, Alex, '"Godfather of AI" Geoffrey Hinton quits Google and warns over dangers of misinformation', *The Guardian,* 2 May 2023, https://www.theguardian.com/technology/2023/may/02/geoffrey-hinton-godfather-of-ai-quits-google-warns-dangers-of-machine-learning

2 Reynoso, Rebecca, 'A Complete History of Artificial Intelligence', *G2,* 25 May 2021, https://www.g2.com/articles/history-of-artificial-intelligence

3 Turing, Alan M., 'Computing Machinery and Intelligence', *Mind* (49: 433-460), 1950, accessed via https://redirect.cs.umbc.edu/courses/471/papers/turing.pdf

4 Oppy, Graham, & Dowe, David, 'The Turing Test', *The Stanford Encyclopedia of Philosophy,* 2021, https://plato.stanford.edu/cgi-bin/encyclopedia/archinfo.cgi?entry=turing-test

5 Anyoha, Rockwell, 'The History of Artificial Intelligence', *Harvard University Blogs,* 28 August 2017, https://sitn.hms.harvard.edu/flash/2017/history-artificial-intelligence/

6 Ibid.

7 Press, Gil, 'A Very Short History of Artificial Intelligence (AI)', *Forbes,* 30 December 2016, https://www.forbes.com/sites/gilpress/2016/12/30/a-very-short-history-of-artificial-intelligence-ai/?sh=680cdbb66fba

8 Vinge, Verner, 'The Coming Technological Singularity: How to Survive in the Post-Human Era', *Whole Earth Review,* 1993, https://www.researchgate.net/publication/283678547_The_Coming_Technological_Singularity

9 History.com editors, 'Deep Blue defeats Garry Kasparov in a Chess Match', *A&E Television Networks,* 16 November 2009, https://www.history.com/this-day-in-history/deep-blue-defeats-garry-kasparov-in-chess-match

10 Britannica, the Editors of Encyclopaedia, 'Moore's Law', *Encyclopaedia Britannica,* 29 September 2023, https://www.britannica.com/technology/Moores-law

11 Garun, Natt, 'How to enable and use Gmail's AI-powered Smart Reply and Smart Compose tools', *The Verge,* 6 July 2020, https://www.theverge.com/21315189/gmail-ai-smart-reply-compose-tools-enable-turn-on-how-to

12 Malik, Aisha, 'Google's new 'multisearch' feature lets you search using text and images at the same time', *TechCrunch,* 7 April 2022, https://techcrunch.com/2022/04/07/googles-multisearch-search-using-text-images/

13 Sha, Arjun, '18 Examples of AI You're Using in Daily Life in 2023', *Beebom,* 29 April 2023, https://beebom.com/examples-of-artificial-intelligence/

14 Samsung Newsroom, 'New Food AI Looks Inside Your Fridge To Help You Find The Perfect Things To Cook With What You ALREADY Have', *Samsung,* 7 January 2020, https://news.samsung.com/us/new-food-ai-looks-inside-fridge-help-find-perfect-things-cook-already/

15 Diaz, Maria, 'The first GPT-powered smart home platform is here', *ZDNet,* 27 June 2023, https://www.zdnet.com/article/the-first-gpt-powered-smart-home-platform-is-here/

16 Meyersohn, Nathaniel, 'Nobody likes self-checkout. Here's why it's everywhere', *CNN Business,* 10 July 2022, https://edition.cnn.com/2022/07/09/business/self-checkout-retail/index.html

17 Des Georges, Colette, '25 stats about AI in customer experience that show how consumers really feel',

SurveyMonkey, n.d., https://www.surveymonkey.com/curiosity/25-stats-about-ai-in-customer-experience-that-show-how-consumers-really-feel/

18 Lloyds Bank, 'Meet our virtual assistant', *Lloyds Bank,* 2023, https://www.lloydsbank.com/contact-us/virtual-assistant.html

19 Natwest, 'Meet Cora, your digital assistant', *NatWest,* 2023, *https://www.natwest.com/business/support-centre/cora.html*

20 Saha, Shritama, 'RIP, human customer service', *Analytics India Magazine,* 18 July 2023, https://analyticsindiamag.com/rip-human-customer-service/

21 Ibid.

22 Plumber, Libby, 'This is how Netflix's top-secret recommendation system works', *Wired,* 22 August 2017, https://www.wired.co.uk/article/how-do-netflixs-algorithms-work-machine-learning-helps-to-predict-what-viewers-will-like

23 Logg, Jennifer M., Minson, Julia A., & Moore, Don A., 'Algorithmic Appreciation: People prefer algorithmic to human judgement', *Organizational Behavior and Human Decision Processes* (151: 90-103), March 2019, https://www.sciencedirect.com/science/article/abs/pii/S0749597818303388

24 Wright, Danny, 'Pop Songs Really Are Shorter Than Ever Now', *Vice,* 13 April 2023, https://www.vice.com/en/article/qjv8pq/pop-songs-shorter-than-ever

25 Beaumont-Thomas, Ben, & Snapes, Laura, 'Has 10 years of Spotify ruined music?', *The Guardian,* 5 October 2018, https://www.theguardian.com/music/2018/oct/05/10-years-of-spotify-should-we-celebrate-or-despair

26 Kleinman, Zoe, 'Spotify will not ban AI-made music, says boss', *BBC News,* 26 September 2023, https://www.bbc.co.uk/news/technology-66882414

27 Zuboff, Shoshana, *The Age of Surveillance Capitalism* (London: Profile Books, 2019)

28 Anderson, Stephen R., 'How many languages are there in the world?', *Linguistic Society of America,* 2010, https://www.linguisticsociety.org/content/how-many-languages-are-there-world

29 Boulter, Liz, 'Three-quarters of UK adults can't read a map – here's how to get better', *The Guardian,* 13 July 2022, https://www.theguardian.com/travel/2022/jul/13/three-quarters-of-uk-adults-cant-read-a-map-heres-how-to-get-better-ordnance-survey-study

30 Gonzales-Franco, Mar, Dane Clemeson, Gregory, & Miller, Amos, 'How GPS Weakens Memory – and What We Can Do about It', *Scientific American,* 7 May 2021, https://www.scientificamerican.com/article/how-gps-weakens-memory-mdash-and-what-we-can-do-about-it/

31 Popa, Bogdan, 'Replacing Google Maps With Traditional Maps Could Help Fight Dementia', *Autoevolution,* 24 January 2023, https://www.autoevolution.com/news/replacing-google-maps-with-traditional-maps-could-help-fight-dementia-209034.html

32 Sha, Arjun, '18 Examples'.

33 BBC News, 'French Open 2023: Grand Slam using AI to protect players from online abuse', *BBC News,* 28 May 2023, https://www.bbc.co.uk/sport/tennis/65706479

34 Ibid.

35 Shieber, Jonathan, 'White Castle rolls out more robots from Miso Robotics to cook in its kitchens', *TechCrunch,* 27 October 2020, https://techcrunch.com/2020/10/27/white-castle-rolls-out-more-robots-from-miso-robotics-to-cook-in-its-kitchens/

36 Dizikes, Peter, 'How many jobs do robots really replace?', *MIT News Office,* 4 May 2020, https://news.mit.edu/2020/how-many-jobs-robots-replace-0504

37 Ibid.

38 Ibid.

39 Nucleus AI, 'The Future of Work: Jobs AI Can and Can't Replace', *YourStory,* 18 May 2023, https://yourstory.com/2023/05/ai-future-of-work-job-automation

40 Japan Times, 'As farmers gray, Japan pins hopes on robots and smart agriculture', *Japan Times,* 25 September 2023, https://www.japantimes.co.jp/business/2023/09/25/economy/japan-smart-agriculture/

41 Ibid.

42 Carey, Peter, 'Introducing… Xihelm, the agri-tech startup leading the UK with Oxford Capital', *IFA Magazine,* 27 May 2021, https://ifamagazine.com/introducing-xihelm-an-agri-tech-startup-shaping-the-uk-industry/

43 Guendelsberger, Emily, 'I Worked at an Amazon Fulfillment Center; They Treat Workers Like Robots', *Time Magazine,* 18 July 2019, https://time.com/5629233/amazon-warehouse-employee-treatment-robots/

44 Liao, Shannon, 'Amazon warehouse workers skip bathroom breaks to keep their jobs, says report', *The Verge,* 16 April 2018, https://www.theverge.com/2018/4/16/17243026/amazon-warehouse-jobs-worker-conditions-bathroom-breaks

45 Paul, Andrew, 'Self-driving taxis get the greenlight on 24/7 service in San Francisco', *PopSci,* 11 August 2023, https://www.popsci.com/technology/san-francisco-robotaxis-public/

46 Chin, Monica, 'Who is responsible when a self-driving car kills someone?', *Mashable,* 22 March 2018, https://mashable.com/article/self-driving-car-fatality-uber-liability

47 Ibid.

48 Capraro, Joe, 'GM's Super Cruise Vs Tesla's Autopilot –

Which Would You Trust To Take The Wheel', *Slashgear via Microsoft Network,* 20 September 2023, https://www.msn.com/en-us/autos/news/gms-super-cruise-vs-teslas-autopilot-which-would-you-trust-to-take-the-wheel/ar-AA1gZgyd

49 Rosenthal, Emily, 'When a Tesla on Autopilot Kills Someone, Who Is Responsible?', *New York University News,* 9 March 2022, https://www.nyu.edu/about/news-publications/news/2022/march/when-a-tesla-on-auto-pilot-kills-someone--who-is-responsible--.html

50 Brownwell, Bradley, 'Elon Musk Wanted To Record Drivers In Attempt To Absolve Tesla Of Fault', *Jalopnik via Microsoft Network,* https://www.msn.com/en-us/autos/news/elon-musk-wanted-to-record-drivers-in-attempt-to-absolve-tesla-of-fault/ar-AA1gX3sx#image=AA1cY43w|1

51 Landymore, Frank, 'Elon Musk stormed into the Tesla office furious that autopilot tried to kill him', *The Byte,* 16 September 2023, https://futurism.com/the-byte/elon-musk-furious-autopilot-tried-kill-him

52 Krisher, Tom, 'Tesla is allowing no-hands driving with autopilot for longer periods. US regulators have questions', *ABC News,* 30 August 2023, https://abcnews.go.com/Technology/wireStory/after-tesla-relaxes-monitoring-drivers-autopilot-technology-us-102671173

53 Ibid.

54 Barrett, Eamon, 'Google says its A.I.-powered flood prediction tool can now issue forecasts 7 days in advance, up from 47 hours', *Fortune Magazine,* 9 November 2022, https://fortune.com/2022/11/08/google-ai-global-flood-hub-prediction-tool/

55 Bastani, Aaron, 'Downstream: God-like AI Is Closer Than You Think w/ Ian Hogarth', *Novara Media,* 22 May 2023, https://podfollow.com/novaramedia/episode/e1e15149d776a036eded1e7a83741cf4979c3df7/view

56 Sample, Ian, 'Google DeepMind AI tool assesses DNA

mutations for harm potential', *The Guardian,* 19 September 2023, https://www.theguardian.com/science/2023/sep/19/ google-deepmind-ai-tool-assesses-dna-mutations-for-harm-potential

57 Singh, Maanvi, 'Elon Musk's Neuralink approved to recruit humans for brain-implant trial', 20 September 2023, https://www.theguardian.com/technology/2023/ sep/19/elon-musk-neuralink-human-trials-brain-implant?C-MP=Share_iOSApp_Other

58 Rouse, Margaret, 'Large Language Model (LLM)', *Techopedia,* 28 July 2023, https://www.techopedia.com/ definition/34948/large-language-model-llm

59 Lutkevich, Ben, 'natural language processing (NLP)', *TechTarget,* January 2023, https://www.techtarget.com/ searchenterpriseai/definition/natural-language-processing-NLP

60 Harris, Mark, 'Elon Musk used to say he put $100M into OpenAI, but now it's $50M: Here are the receipts', *TechCrunch,* 18 May 2023, https://techcrunch. com/2023/05/17/elon-musk-used-to-say-he-put-100m-in-openai-but-now-its-50m-here-are-the-receipts/?guc-counter=1&guce_referrer=aHR0cHM6Ly9lbi53aWtppc-GVkaWEub3JnLw&guce_referrer_sig=AQAAACqRRg6iK-cJ8wEUOWe6lV8csWSJaebL204xOO3Utol7MFlFHm-biXy_8u-v0UfE39sm-MUHcxcAkNDppKx8HuXgjuxe-fn-pm0FOsXpH496mGuismXyjYDLaRuQc5KhKOs4undHg-bRogaclUZIbeL0RWLbCTGivF-cEH9MLa4glurH

61 OpenAI, 'Creating safe AGI that benefits all of humanity', *OpenAI,* 2023, https://openai.com/

62 Arunasalam, Samrhitha, 'ChatGPT users can now browse internet, OpenAI says', *Reuters,* 28 September 2023, https:// www.reuters.com/technology/openai-says-chatgpt-can-now-browse-internet-2023-09-27/

63 Sheen, Tom, 'DALL-E', Techopedia, 23 March 2023,

https://www.techopedia.com/definition/dall-e

64 Shead, Sam, 'How DeepMind convinced billionaire Peter Thiel to invest without moving the company to Silicon Valley', *Business Insider*, 18 July 2017, https://www.businessinsider.com/how-deepmind-convinced-peter-thiel-to-invest-outside-silicon-valley-2017-7?r=US&IR=T; Cuthbertson, Anthony, 'Elon Musk: Artificial Intelligence 'Potentially More Dangerous than Nukes'', *International Business Times*, https://www.ibtimes.co.uk/elon-musk-artificial-intelligence-potentially-more-dangerous-nukes-1459710

65 Sweney, Mark, 'Amazon to invest up to $4bn in OpenAI rival Anthropic', *The Guardian*, 25 September 2023, https://www.theguardian.com/technology/2023/sep/25/amazon-invest-openai-rival-anthropic-microsoft-chat-gpt?CMP=Share_iOSApp_Other

66 Metz, Rachel, & McBride, Sarah, 'Elon Musk Announces New Company xAI as He Seeks to Build ChatGPT Alternative', *Bloomberg*, 12 July 2023, https://www.bloomberg.com/news/articles/2023-07-12/musk-unveils-xai-as-way-to-understand-true-nature-of-universe?leadSource=uverify%20wall

67 Reuters, 'Elon Musk says xAI will use public tweets for AI model training', *Reuters via Yahoo! Finance*, 14 July 2023, https://finance.yahoo.com/news/elon-musk-says-xai-public-210338600.html?guccounter=1

68 Hertzmann, Aaron, 'Give this AI a few words of description and it produces a stunning image – but is it art?', *The Conversation*, 10 June 2022, https://theconversation.com/give-this-ai-a-few-words-of-description-and-it-produces-a-stunning-image-but-is-it-art-184363

69 Vincent, James, 'The swagged-out pope is an AI fake – and an early glimpse of a new reality', *The Verge*, 27 March 2023, https://www.theverge.com/2023/3/27/23657927/ai-pope-image-fake-midjourney-computer-generated-aesthetic

70 Konrad, Alex, 'Inflection AI, Startup from Ex-DeepMind Leaders, Launches Pi – A Chattier Chatbot', *Forbes,* 2 May 2023, https://www.forbes.com/sites/alexkonrad/2023/05/02/inflection-ai-ex-deepmind-launches-pi-chatbot/

71 Starks Jr, Rob, 'Microsoft: A long term investment in AI', *The Motley Fool,* 8 August 2023, https://www.fool.com/investing/2023/08/08/microsoft-a-long-term-investment-in-ai/

72 Waters, Dustin, 'The historic chess showdown between man and AI, decades before ChatGPT', *The Washington Post,* 22 May 2023, https://www.washingtonpost.com/history/2023/05/22/garry-kasparov-chess-deep-blue-ibm/

73 Wiggers, Kyle, 'IBM rolls out new generative AI features and models', *TechCrunch,* 7 September 2023, https://techcrunch.com/2023/09/07/ibm-rolls-out-new-generative-ai-features-and-models/

74 Goldman, Sharon, 'How Nvidia dominated AI – and plans to keep it that way as generative AI explodes', *VentureBeat,* 23 February 2023, https://venturebeat.com/ai/how-nvidia-dominated-ai-and-plans-to-keep-it-that-way-as-generative-ai-explodes/

75 Mehta, Ivan, 'Adobe launches Photoshop's web version with Firefly-powered AI tools', *TechCrunch,* 28 September 2023, https://techcrunch.com/2023/09/28/adobe-launches-photoshops-web-version-with-firefly-powered-ai-tools/

76 Griffin, Andrew, 'Lensa AI: Tool that turns your photos into stunning portraits hit by growing criticism', *The Independent,* 9 December 2022, https://www.independent.co.uk/tech/lensa-ai-photo-portrait-app-download-how-to-b2242408.html

77 Kleinman, Zoe, & Vallance, Chris, 'AI 'godfather' Geoffrey Hinton warns of dangers as he quits Google', *BBC News,* 2 May 2023, https://www.bbc.co.uk/news/world-us-canada-65452940

78 Bastani, 'Downstream'.

79 Idbrahim, Mohamed, 'Unraveling the Evolution: Chat-GPT, GPT-3, GPT-3.5, and GPT-4 – What's New?', *Bright Coding,* 17 March 2023, https://www.blog.brightcoding.dev/2023/03/17/unraveling-the-evolution-chatgpt-gpt-3-gpt-3-5-and-gpt-4-whats-new/

80 Roberts, Greg [AcroYogi], 'AI 101: What is a Parameter? (in a Chatbot LLM)', *Musings of Freedom,* 6 March 2023, https://gregoreite.com/ai-101-what-is-a-parameter-in-a-chat-bot-llm/

81 Popovic, Matt, 'ChatGPT Parameters Explained: A Deep Dive into the World of NLP', *EcoAgi,* 5 June 2023, https://ecoagi.ai/articles/chatgpt-parameters

82 Weiss, Debra Cassens, 'Latest version of ChatGPT aces bar exam with core nearing 90th percentile', *American Bar Association (ABA) Journal,* 16 March 2023, https://www.abajournal.com/web/article/latest-version-of-chatgpt-aces-the-bar-exam-with-score-in-90th-percentile

83 Parshall, Allison, 'Music-Making Artificial Intelligence Is Getting Scary Good', *Scientific American,* 24 March 2023, https://www.scientificamerican.com/podcast/episode/music-making-artificial-intelligence-is-getting-scary-good/

84 Martindale, Jon, 'GPT-4 vs. GPT-3.5: how much difference in there?', *digitaltrends,* 28 April 2023, https://www.digitaltrends.com/computing/gpt-4-vs-gpt-35/

85 Thorbecke, Catherine, 'Now you can talk to ChatGPT – and it will talk back', *CNN Business,* 25 September 2023, https://edition.cnn.com/2023/09/25/tech/chatgpt-open-ai-humanlike-update/index.html

86 George, Alexandra, & Walsh, Toby, 'Artificial intelligence is breaking patent law', *Nature,* 24 May 2022, https://www.nature.com/articles/d41586-022-01391-x

87 Alter, Alexandra, & Harris, Elizabeth A., 'Franzen, Grisham and Other Prominent Authors Sue OpenAI', *The*

New York Times, 20 September 2023, https://www.nytimes.com/2023/09/20/books/authors-openai-lawsuit-chatgpt-copyright.html

88 ABC News, 'Author's lawsuit against OpenAI could 'fundamentally reshape' AI: Experts', *ABC News via Microsoft Network,* 25 September 2023, https://www.msn.com/en-us/news/technology/authors-lawsuit-against-openai-could-fundamentally-reshape-ai-experts/ar-AA1hfcuh

89 Vallance, Chris, 'Sarah Silverman sues OpenAI and Meta', *BBC News,* 12 July 2023, https://www.bbc.co.uk/news/technology-66164228

90 Brittain, Blake, 'Thomson Reuters AI copyright dispute must go to trial, judge says', *Reuters via Yahoo! News',* 26 September 2023, https://news.yahoo.com/thomson-reuters-ai-copyright-dispute-004143639.html

91 Chapman, Zoë, 'Changes to the Public Order Act would amount to "draconian" restrictions on the right to protest', *Open Access Government,* 9 June 2023, https://www.openaccessgovernment.org/public-order-act-uk-government-lords-parliament-police/160726/

92 Barradale, Greg, 'UK's civil liberties rating downgraded thanks to government crackdowns on protests, elections and strikes', *The Big Issue,* 16 March 2023, https://www.bigissue.com/news/activism/uks-civil-liberties-rating-downgraded-thanks-to-government-crackdowns-on-protests-elections-and-strikes/

93 Martin, Peter, & Manson, Katrina, 'CIA Builds Its Own Artificial Intelligence Tool in Rivalry with China', *Bloomberg,* 26 September 2023, https://www.bloomberg.com/news/articles/2023-09-26/cia-builds-its-own-artificial-intelligence-tool-in-rivalry-with-china?leadSource=uverify%20wall

94 Mack, Bunny McKensie, 'Systemic Racism in AI: How Algorithms Replicate White Supremacy and Injustice',

TeenVogue via Yahoo! News, 19 September 2023, https://www.yahoo.com/lifestyle/systemic-racism-ai-algorithms-replicate-120000415.html

95 Cumming-Bruce, Nick, 'U.N. Panel: Technology in Policing Can Reinforce Racial Bias', *New York Times,* 7 December 2020, https://www.nytimes.com/2020/11/26/us/un-panel-technology-in-policing-can-reinforce-racial-bias.html

96 Reese, Hope, 'What Happens When Police Use AI to Predict and Prevent Crime?', *JSTOR Daily,* 23 February 2022, https://daily.jstor.org/what-happens-when-police-use-ai-to-predict-and-prevent-crime/

97 Mac, Ryan, 'Facebook Apologizes After A.I. Puts "Primates" Label on Video of Black Men', *New York Times,* 3 September 2021, https://www.nytimes.com/2021/09/03/technology/facebook-ai-race-primates.html

98 Newman, Marissa, 'Israel's new military AI systems select targets and plan missions "in minutes"', *Japan Times,* 17 July 2023, https://www.japantimes.co.jp/news/2023/07/17/world/israel-quietly-embeds-ai-military-systems/

99 Aitken, Peter, 'Israel's new multimillion-dollar AI tank provides total battlefield vision: "A new era"', *Fox News via Yahoo! News,* 22 September 2023, https://news.yahoo.com/israels-multimillion-dollar-ai-tank-090012602.html

100 Stacey, Kiran, & Milmo, Dan, 'No 10 worried AI could be used to create advanced weapons that escape human control', *The Guardian,* 25 September 2023, https://www.theguardian.com/technology/2023/sep/25/ai-bioweapons-rishi-sunak-safety?CMP=Share_iOSApp_Other

101 Prakash, Prarthana, '"The Godfather of A.I." just quit Google and says he regrets his life's work because it can be hard to stop 'bad actors from using it for bad things"', *Fortune Magazine,* 1 May 2023, https://fortune.

com/2023/05/01/godfather-ai-geoffrey-hinton-quit-google-regrets-lifes-work-bad-actors/

102 Dominguez, Gabriel, 'The next arms race: China leverages AI for edge in future wars', *Japan Times,* 20 April 2023, https://www.japantimes.co.jp/news/2023/04/20/asia-pacific/china-ai-future-wars/

103 Hammond, George, 'Alexandr Wang: US technologists should help preserve US military and economic leadership', *The Financial Times,* 13 September 2023, https://www.ft.com/content/98b0a060-0e2e-4001-a4b6-8c388c106988

104 Bergengruen, Vera, 'Tech Leaders Warn the U.S. Military is Falling Behind China on AI', *Time Magazine,* 18 July 2023, https://time.com/6295586/military-ai-warfare-alexandr-wang/

105 Tang, Jerry et al., 'Semantic reconstruction of continuous language from non-invasive brain recordings', *Nature Neuroscience* (26: 858-866), 1 May 2023, https://www.nature.com/articles/s41593-023-01304-9

106 Whang, Oliver, 'A.I. Is Getting Better at Mind-Reading', *The New York Times,* 1 May 2023, https://www.nytimes.com/2023/05/01/science/ai-speech-language.html?smid=nytcore-ios-share&referringSource=articleShare

107 Lawler, Daniel, 'Scientists use brain scans and AI to 'decode' thoughts', *Japan Times,* 2 May 2023, https://www.japantimes.co.jp/news/2023/05/02/world/science-health-world/ai-thought-decoder/

108 Rodriguez, Salvador, Seetharaman, Deepa, & Tilley, Aaron, 'Meta to Push for Younger Users with New AI Chatbot Characters', *The Wall Street Journal,* 24 September 2023, https://www.wsj.com/tech/ai/meta-ai-chatbot-younger-users-dab6cb32

109 Coleman, Theara, 'Can Meta woo Gen Z with AI chatbots?', *The Week,* 25 September 2023, https://theweek.com/tech/meta-gen-z-ai-chatbots

110 Isaac, Mike, & Metz, Cade, 'Meet the A.I. Jane Austen: Meta weaves A.I. Throughout Its Apps', *The New York Times,* 27 September 2023, https://www. nytimes.com/2023/09/27/technology/meta-ai-celebrities. html?smid=nytcore-ios-share&referringSource=articleShare

111 Pearcy, Aimee, '"It was as if my father were actually texting me": grief in the age of AI', *The Guardian,* 18 July 2023, https://www.theguardian.com/technology/2023/jul/18/ ai-chatbots-grief-chatgpt?CMP=Share_iOSApp_Other

112 Lorenz, Taylor, 'An influencer's AI clone will be your girlfriend for $1 a minute', *The Washington Post,* 13 May 2023, https://www.washingtonpost.com/ technology/2023/05/13/caryn-ai-technology-gpt-4/

113 Duggins, Alexi, '"It could have me read porn": Stephen Fry shocked by AI cloning of his voice in documentary', *The Guardian,* 20 September 2023, https://www.theguardian.com/technology/2023/sep/20/ it-could-have-me-read-porn-stephen-fry-shocked-by-ai-clon-ing-of-his-voice-in-documentary

114 Dodd, Vikram, & Milmo, Dan, 'AI could worsen epidemic of child sexual abuse, warns UK crime agency', *The Guardian,* 18 July 2023, https://www.theguardian.com/ society/2023/jul/18/ai-could-worsen-epidemic-of-child-sex-ual-abuse-warns-uk-agency?CMP=Share_iOSApp_Other

115 Weaver, Matthew, 'AI chatbot 'encouraged' man who planned to kill queen, court told', *The Guardian,* 6 July 2023, https://www.theguardian.com/uk-news/2023/jul/06/ ai-chatbot-encouraged-man-who-planned-to-kill-queen-court-told?CMP=Share_iOSApp_Other

116 Piltch, Avram, 'Google's AI Bots Tout 'Benefits' of Genocide, Slavery, Fascism, Other Evils', *Tom's Hardware,* 22 August 2023, https://www.tomshardware.com/news/ google-bots-tout-slavery-genocide

117 Ibid.

118 Milmo, Dan, & Devlin, Hannah, 'AI watch: from deepfakes to a rockstar humanoid', *The Guardian,* 7 July 2023, https://www.theguardian.com/technology/2023/jul/07/ai-watch-deepfakes-humanoid-robot-artificial-intelligence

119 Moran, Chris, 'ChatGPT is making up fake Guardian articles. Here's how we're responding', *The Guardian,* 6 April 2023, https://www.theguardian.com/commentisfree/2023/apr/06/ai-chatgpt-guardian-technology-risks-fake-article?CMP=Share_iOSApp_Other

120 Hsu, Tiffany, & Thompson, Stuart A., 'Disinformation Researchers Raise Alarms About A.I. Chatbots', *The New York Times,* 13 February 2023, https://www.nytimes.com/2023/02/08/technology/ai-chatbots-disinformation.html

121 Klepper, David, 'It turns out that ChatGPT is really good at creating online propaganda: "I think what's clear is that in the wrong hands there's going to be a lot of trouble"', *Fortune Magazine,* 24 January 2023, https://fortune.com/2023/01/24/chatgpt-open-ai-online-propaganda/

122 Arvanitis, Lorenzo, Sadeghi, McKenzie, & Brewster, Jack, 'Despite OpenAI's Promises, the Company's New AI Tool Produces Misinformation More Frequently, and More Persuasively, than its Predecessor', *NewsGuard Tech,* March 2023, https://www.newsguardtech.com/misinformation-monitor/march-2023/

123 Karimi, Faith, '"Mom, these bad men have me": She believes scammers cloned her daughter's voice in a fake kidnapping', *CNN,* 29 April 2023, https://edition.cnn.com/2023/04/29/us/ai-scam-calls-kidnapping-cec/index.html

124 Allyn, Bobby, 'Deepfake video of Zelenskyy could be "tip of the iceberg" in info war, experts warn', *NPR,* 16 March 2022, https://www.npr.org/2022/03/16/1087062648/deepfake-video-zelenskyy-experts-war-manipulation-ukraine-russia

125 Quinn, Ben, & Milmo, Dan, 'Time running out for UK electoral system to keep up with AI, say regulators', *The Guardian,* 28 June 2023, https://www.theguardian.com/politics/2023/jun/28/time-running-out-for-uk-electoral-system-to-keep-up-with-ai?CMP=Share_iOSApp_Other

126 Nobel Prize Outreach AB 2023, 'Maria Ressa – Nobel Prize Lecture', *NobelPrize.org,* 10 December 2021, https://www.nobelprize.org/prizes/peace/2021/ressa/lecture/

127 Kelly, Philippa, 'Ai having "positive impact" on UK jobs but could increase regional inequalities', says report', *The Guardian,* 20 September 2023, https://www.theguardian.com/global-development/2023/sep/20/ai-having-positive-impact-on-uk-jobs-but-could-increase-regional-inequalities-says-report?CMP=Share_iOSApp_Other

128 Diab, Khaled, 'What future for journalism in the age of AI?', *Al Jazeera,* 19 July 2023, https://www.aljazeera.com/opinions/2023/7/19/what-future-for-journalism-in-the-age-of-ai

129 Paul, Kari, 'BuzzFeed to use AI to "enhance" its content and quizzes – report', *The Guardian,* 26 January 2023, https://www.theguardian.com/media/2023/jan/26/buzzfeed-artifical-intelligence-content-quizzes-chatgpt?CMP=Share_iOSApp_Other

130 Economic Times, 'India welcomes its first regional AI news anchor, "Lisa"', *The Economic Times,* 13 July 2023, https://economictimes.indiatimes.com/news/new-updates/india-welcomes-is-first-regional-ai-news-anchor-lisa/articleshow/101659464.cms?from=mdr

131 Wakefield, Jake, 'Intelligent Machines: The jobs robots will steal first', *BBC News,* 14 September 2015, https://www.bbc.co.uk/news/technology-33327659

132 Hatzius, Jan, et al., 'The Potentially Large Effects of Artificial Intelligence on Economic Growth', *Goldman Sachs,* 26 March 2023, https://www.key4biz.it/wp-content/

uploads/2023/03/Global-Economics-Analyst_-The-Poten-
tially-Large-Effects-of-Artificial-Intelligence-on-Econom-
ic-Growth-Briggs_Kodnani.pdf

133 Ibid.

134 Eloundou, Tyna, et al., 'GPTs are GPTs: An Early
Look at the Labour Market Impact Potential of Large
Language Models', *The University of Pennsylvania, Open
Research, and OpenAI,* 22 August 2023, https://arxiv.org/
pdf/2303.10130.pdf

135 Digalaki, Eleni, 'The impact of artificial intelligence
in the banking sector & how AI is being used in 2023',
Business Insider, 2 February 2022, https://www.businessin-
sider.com/ai-in-banking-report?r=US&IR=T

136 Ibid.

137 He, David, & Guo, Vanessa, '4 ways AI will
impact the financial job market', *The World Economic
Forum,* 14 September 2018, https://www.weforum.org/
agenda/2018/09/4-ways-ai-artificial-intelligence-impact-fi-
nancial-job-market/

138 Perlman, Andrew M., 'The Implications of ChatGPT for
Legal Services and Society', 5 December 2022, https://ssrn.
com/abstract=4294197

139 Espiner, Tom, 'BT to cut 55,000 jobs with up to a fifth
replaced by AI', *BBC News,* 18 May 2023, https://www.bbc.
co.uk/news/business-65631168

140 Ford, Brody, 'IBM to Pause Hiring for All Jobs
That AI Could Do', *Bloomberg,* 1 May 2023, https://
www.bloomberg.com/news/articles/2023-05-01/
ibm-to-pause-hiring-for-back-office-jobs-that-ai-could-
kill?leadSource=uverify%20wall

141 Bastani, 'Downstream'.

142 Roose, Kevin, 'Bing's A.I. Chat: "I Want to Be Alive"',
The New York Times, 17 February 2023, https://www.

nytimes.com/2023/02/16/technology/bing-chatbot-transcript.
html?smid=nytcore-ios-share&referringSource=articleShare

143 Bastani, 'Downstream'.

144 Coulter, Martin, 'AI pioneer says its threat to world
may be "more urgent" than climate change', *Reuters,*
9 May 2023, https://www.reuters.com/technology/
ai-pioneer-says-its-threat-world-may-be-more-urgent-than-
climate-change-2023-05-05/

145 Streitfeld, David, 'Silicon Valley Confronts the Idea
That the 'Singularity' Is Here', *The New York TImes,* 11 June
2023, https://www.nytimes.com/2023/06/11/technology/
silicon-valley-confronts-the-idea-that-the-singularity-is-here.
html?smid=nytcore-ios-share&referringSource=article-
Share11

146 Ibid.

147 Ibid.

148 Bastani, 'Downstream'.

149 Ibid.

150 Whang, Oliver, 'How to Tell if Your A.I. is Conscious',
New York Times, 18 September 2023, https://www.nytimes.
com/2023/09/18/science/ai-computers-consciousness.html

151 Fassihi, Farnaz, 'U.N. Officials Urge Regulation
of Artificial Intelligence', *The New York Times,* 18 July
2023, https://www.nytimes.com/2023/07/18/world/
un-security-council-ai.html?smid=nytcore-ios-share&refer-
ringSource=articleShare

152 EU Parliament, 'EU AI Act: first regulation on
artificial intelligence', *European Parliament,* 8 June
2023, https://www.europarl.europa.eu/news/en/headlines/
society/20230601STO93804/eu-ai-act-first-regulation-on-ar-
tificial-intelligence

153 AI Now Institute, Kak, Amba, & West, Sarah Myers,
'General Purpose AI Poses Serious Risks, Should Not Be

Excluded From the EU's AI Act | Policy Brief', *AI Now,* 13 April 2023, https://ainowinstitute.org/publication/gpai-is-high-risk-should-not-be-excluded-from-eu-ai-act

154 Stewart, Heather, 'Calls for stricter UK oversight of workplace AI amid fears for staff rights', *The Guardian,* 16 April 2023, https://www.theguardian.com/law/2023/apr/16/calls-stricter-oversight-workplace-ai-fears-staff-rights?CMP=Share_iOSApp_Other

155 Milmo, Dan, 'Dangerous AI systems need a "smoke alarm" warn UK ministers', *The Guardian,* 25 September 2023, https://www.theguardian.com/technology/2023/sep/25/dangerous-ai-systems-need-a-smoke-alarm-warn-ministers?CMP=Share_iOSApp_Other

156 Stacey, Kiran, 'AI should be licensed like medicine or nuclear power, Labour suggests', *The Guardian,* 5 June 2023, https://www.theguardian.com/technology/2023/jun/05/ai-could-outwit-humans-in-two-years-says-uk-government-adviser?CMP=Share_iOSApp_Other

157 The White House, 'FACT SHEET: Biden-Harris Administration Secures Voluntary Commitments from Leading Artificial Intelligence Companies to Manage the Risks Posed by AI', *White House Briefing Room,* 21 July 2023, https://www.whitehouse.gov/briefing-room/statements-releases/2023/07/21/fact-sheet-biden-harris-administration-secures-voluntary-commitments-from-leading-artificial-intelligence-companies-to-manage-the-risks-posed-by-ai/

158 Moss, Sebastian, 'Microsoft's water consumption jumps 34 percent amid AI boom', *Data Center Dynamics,* 12 September 2023, https://www.datacenterdynamics.com/en/news/microsofts-water-consumption-jumps-34-percent-amid-ai-boom/

159 Bastani, 'Downstream'.

160 Bianchi, Tiago, 'Market share of leading search engines

in the United Kingdom (UK) in April 2023', *Statista,* 20 September 2023, https://www.statista.com/statistics/280269/market-share-held-by-search-engines-in-the-united-kingdom/

161 Clifford, Catherine, 'Mark Cuban: The world's first trillionaire will be an artificial intelligence entrepreneur', *CNBC,* 13 March 2017, https://www.cnbc.com/2017/03/13/mark-cuban-the-worlds-first-trillionaire-will-be-an-ai-entrepreneur.html

162 Allen, Mike, 'Employers trusted more than government', *Axios,* 16 January 2023, https://www.axios.com/2023/01/16/edelman-trust-employers-government-survey

163 Henley, Jon, 'Younger people more likely to doubt merits of democracy – global poll', *The Guardian,* 11 September 2023, https://www.theguardian.com/world/2023/sep/11/younger-people-more-relaxed-alternatives-democracy-survey

164 Cadwalladr, Carole, "Capitalism is dead. Now we have something much worse': Yanis Varoufakis on extremism, Starmer, and the tyranny of big tech', *The Guardian,* 24 September 2023, https://www.theguardian.com/world/2023/sep/24/yanis-varoufakis-technofeudalism-capitalism-ukraine-interview?CMP=Share_iOSApp_Other

165 Goodreads, 'Player Piano', *Goodreads,* 2023, https://www.goodreads.com/en/book/show/9597

166 The Equality Trust, 'The Scale of Economic Inequality in the UK', *The Equality Trust,* 2023, https://equalitytrust.org.uk/scale-economic-inequality-uk

167 Jones, Josh, 'When John Maynard Keynes Predicted a 15-hour Workweek "in a Hundred Years Time" (1930)', *Open Culture,* 16th June 2020, https://www.openculture.com/2020/06/when-john-maynard-keynes-predicted-a-15-hour-workweek-in-a-hundred-years-time-1930.html

BOOK CLUB DISCUSSION GUIDE

—

First, did you enjoy *The Little Black Book of Artificial Intelligence*? Let us know on Twitter, X or whatever it's called by the time you read this:

Kyle is @kyletaylor

Byline Books is @BylineTimes

Second, do you want to discuss it with friends and family but they need to read it first? The book will always be available at littleblackaibook.com

Third, here are some questions to get conversation started:

1. What was your initial reaction to the book? Shock? Disbelief? "I told you so?"

2. The author attempts to categorise different types of artificial intelligence to bring more nuance to the debate around its impact on humanity. What do you think of the categories? Helpful? Wrong?

3. Government's failures to reign in the power of big tech companies that provide social media and search, like Facebook and Google, are

used as a warning sign for issues surrounding AI. Is that a good example? Do you think these two things are relatable or too different to be a reasonable comparison?

4. The author suggested that we need to develop and use a new language to describe artificial intelligence. How did reading the description of AI using his suggested phrasing change the way you related to the concepts discussed?

5. The author notes a trend among people of having more trust in corporations than nonprofits, governments or the media, which can make it more difficult to make the case for public interest AI development. Do you share this sentiment? If so or if not, what examples can you think of that make your point?

6. Where do you think we'll be five years from now? Discuss (over wine, ideally).

ABOUT THE AUTHOR

Kyle Taylor is the creator of the Little Black Book series. The Little Black Book of Artificial Intelligence is his fifth book and the fourth in the Little Black Book series.

Kyle is the founder of Fair Vote UK and a leading campaigner on election integrity and digital democracy issues, including regulation of social media and artificial intelligence. He has advised governments and campaigners around the world on these issues. He is the former campaign director and chief of staff to a UK government minister and has worked on half a dozen election campaigns in the UK and the USA, including the 2016 US Presidential Campaign.

He is a graduate of American University and the London School of Economics. Kyle is currently a visiting Fellow at the Peace Centre in Tokyo, Japan where his work is focused on the impact of social media and artificial intelligence on human rights and democratic systems.

Other titles by Kyle Taylor:

The Little Black Book of Data and Democracy

The Little Black Book of Lying Boris Johnson

The Little Black Book of Social Media

Exploring Cyberspace (Published by HarperCollins)